World of Dance

Middle Eastern Dance

SECOND EDITION

World of Dance

World of Dance

Middle Eastern Dance

SECOND EDITION

Penni AlZayer

Consulting editor:
Elizabeth A. Hanley,
Associate Professor
Emerita of Kinesiology,
Penn State University

Foreword by
Jacques D'Amboise,
Founder of the National
Dance Institute

CHELSEA HOUSE
PUBLISHERS
An imprint of Infobase Publishing

World of Dance: Middle Eastern Dance, Second Edition

Copyright © 2010 by Infobase Publishing

Chelsea House
An imprint of Infobase Publishing
132 West 31st Street
New York NY 10001

Library of Congress Cataloging-in-Publication Data
AlZayer, Penni.
  Middle Eastern dance / Penni AlZayer. — 2nd ed.
    p. cm.
  Includes bibliographical references and index.
  ISBN 978-1-60413-482-7 (hardcover)
  1. Dance—Middle East. 2. Dance—Arab Countries. I. Title.

GV1704.A52 2010
793.3'1953—dc22   2009041333

Chelsea House books are available at special discounts when purchased in bulk quantities for businesses, associations, institutions, or sales promotions. Please call our Special Sales Department in New York at (212) 967-8800 or (800) 322-8755.

You can find Chelsea House on the World Wide Web at
http://www.chelseahouse.com

Text design by Kerry Casey
Cover design by Alicia Post
Composition by EJB Publishing Services
Cover printed by Bang Printing, Brainerd, Minn.
Book printed and bound by Bang Printing, Brainerd, Minn.
Date printed: March 2010
Printed in the United States of America

10 9 8 7 6 5 4 3 2 1

This book is printed on acid-free paper.

All links and Web addresses were checked and verified to be correct at the time of publication. Because of the dynamic nature of the Web, some addresses and links may have changed since publication and may no longer be valid.

CONTENTS

INTRODUCTION

The world of dance is yours to enjoy! Dance has existed from time immemorial. It has been an integral part of celebrations and rituals, a means of communication with gods and among humans, and a basic source of enjoyment and beauty.

Dance is a fundamental element of human behavior and has evolved over the years from primitive movement of the earliest civilizations to traditional ethnic or folk styles, to the classical ballet and modern dance genres popular today. The term *dance* is broad and, therefore, not limited to the genres noted above. In the twenty-first century, dance includes ballroom, jazz, tap, aerobics, and a myriad of other movement activities. The joy derived from participating in dance of any genre and the physical activity required provide the opportunity for the pursuit of a healthy lifestyle in today's world.

The richness of cultural traditions observed in the ethnic, or folk, dance genre offers the participant, as well as the spectator, insight into the customs, geography, dress, and religious nature of a particular people. Originally passed on from one generation to the next, many ethnic, or folk, dances continue to evolve as our civilization and society change. From these quaint beginnings of traditional dance, a new genre emerged as a way to appeal to the upper level of society: ballet. This new form of dance rose quickly in popularity and remains so today. The genre of ethnic, or folk, dance continues to be an important part of ethnic communities throughout the United States, particularly in large cities.

When the era of modern dance emerged as a contrast and a challenge to the rigorously structured world of ballet, it was not readily accepted as an art form. Modern dance was interested in the communication of emotional experiences—through basic movement, as well as uninhibited movement—not through the academic tradition of ballet masters. Modern dance, however, found its aficionados and is a popular art form today.

No dance form is permanent, definitive, or ultimate. Changes occur, but the basic element of dance endures. Dance is for all people. One need only recall that dance needs neither common race nor common language for communication; it has been, and remains, a universal means of communication.

The WORLD OF DANCE series provides a starting point for readers interested in learning about ethnic, or folk, dances of world cultures, as well as the art forms of ballet and modern dance. This series features an overview of the development of these dance genres, from a historical perspective to a practical one. Highlighting specific cultures, their dance steps and movements, and their customs and traditions underscores the importance of these fundamental elements for the reader. Ballet and modern dance—more recent artistic dance genres—are explored in detail as well, giving the reader a comprehensive knowledge of their past, present, and potential future of each dance form.

The one fact that each reader should remember is that dance has always been, and always will be, a form of communication. This is its legacy to the world.

***

Author Penni AlZayer delves into the fascinating history of the Middle East, native dances of the area, and religious influences on these dances. AlZayer also provides, in the final section, examples of Middle Eastern dance movements for the reader to explore on his/her own.

AlZayer notes that the Middle East is a region with some of the oldest and richest civilizations of the world and that many of the dances associated with the region have endured for centuries. She includes in her discussion the dances of North Africa, as well as the Western "Orientalist" interpretation of Middle Eastern dance and its inaccuracies, mostly with regard to *belly dance*. While belly dance may be one of the region's best-known exports, AlZayer demonstrates that the Middle East has a wide array of other vibrant dances, some with religious significance (e.g., the dance of the Whirling Dervishes of Turkey) and some that are secular (e.g., the dabkeh of the Levant).

Throughout this book, AlZayer takes great care to highlight the purpose, costumes, and music associated with each dance tradition, and in so doing, she sheds light on the legends and mystery surrounding the region once known as "the Orient."

—Elizabeth A. Hanley
Associate Professor Emerita of Kinesiology at
Pennsylvania State University

FOREWORD

*In song and dance, man expresses himself as a member of
a higher community. He forgets how to walk and speak
and is on the way into flying into the air, dancing. . . .
His very gestures express enchantment.*

—Friedrich Nietzsche

In a conversation with George Balanchine [one of the twentieth century's most famous choreographers and the cofounder of the New York City Ballet] discussing the definition of dance, we evolved the following description: "Dance is an expression of time and space, using the control of movement and gesture to communicate."

Dance is central to the human being's expression of emotion. Every time we shake someone's hand, lift a glass in a toast, wave good-bye, or applaud a performer, we are doing a form of dance. We live in a universe of time and space, and dance is an art form invented by human beings to express and convey emotions. Dance is profound.

There are melodies that, when played, will cause your heart to droop with sadness for no known reason. Or a rousing jig or mazurka will have your foot tapping in an accompanying rhythm, seemingly beyond your control. The emotions, contacted through music, spur the body to react physically. Our bodies have just been programmed to express emotions. We dance for many reasons: for religious rituals from the most ancient times; for dealing with sadness, tearfully swaying and holding hands at a wake; for celebrating weddings, joyfully spinning in circles; for entertainment; for dating and mating. How many millions of couples through the ages have said, "We met at a dance"? But most of all, we dance for joy, often exclaiming, "How I love to dance!" Oh, the JOY OF DANCE!

I was teaching dance at a boarding school for emotionally disturbed children, ages 9 through 16. They were participating with 20 other schools in the National Dance Institute's (NDI) year-round program. The boarding school children had been traumatized in frightening and mind-boggling ways. There were a dozen students in my class, and the average attention span may have been 15 seconds—which made for a raucous bunch. This was a tough class.

One young boy, an 11-year-old, was an exception. He never took his eyes off of me for the 35 minutes of the dance class, and they were blazing blue eyes—electric, set in a chalk-white face. His body was slim, trim, superbly proportioned, and he stood arrow-straight. His lips were clamped in a rigid, determined line as he learned and executed every dance step with amazing skill. His concentration was intense despite the wild cavorting, noise, and otherwise disruptive behavior supplied by his fellow classmates.

At the end of class, I went up to him and said, "Wow, can you dance. You're great! What's your name?"

Those blue eyes didn't blink. Then he parted his rigid lips and bared his teeth in a grimace that may have been a smile. He had a big hole where his front teeth should be. I covered my shock and didn't let it show. Both top and bottom incisors had been worn away by his continual grinding and rubbing of them together. One of the supervisors of the school rushed over to me and said, "Oh, his name is Michael. He's very intelligent, but he doesn't speak."

I heard Michael's story from the supervisor. Apparently, when he was a toddler in his playpen, he witnessed his father shooting his mother; then putting the gun to his own head, the father killed himself. It was close to three days before the neighbors broke in to find the dead and swollen bodies of his parents. The dehydrated and starving little boy was stuck in his playpen, sitting in his own filth. The orphaned Michael disappeared into the foster care system, eventually ending up in the boarding school. No one had ever heard him speak.

In the ensuing weeks of dance class, I built and developed choreography for Michael and his classmates. In the spring, they were scheduled to dance in a spectacular NDI show called *The Event of the Year*. At the boarding school, I used Michael as the leader and as a model for the others and began welding all of the kids together, inventing a vigorous and energetic dance to utilize their explosive energy. It took awhile, but they were coming together, little by little over the months. And through all that time, the best in the class—the determined and concentrating Michael—never spoke.

That spring, dancers from the 22 different schools with which the NDI had dance programs were scheduled to come together at Madison Square Garden for *The Event of the Year*. There would be more than 2,000 dancers, a symphony orchestra, a jazz orchestra, a chorus, Broadway stars, narrators, and Native American Indian drummers. There was scenery that was the length of an entire city block and visiting guest children from six foreign countries coming to dance with our New York City children. All of these elements had to come together and fit into a spectacular performance, with only one day of rehearsal. The foremost challenge was how to get 2,000 dancing children on stage for the opening number.

At NDI, we have developed a system called "the runs." First, we divide the stage into a grid with colored lines making the outlines of box shapes, making a mosaic of patterns and shapes on the stage floor. Each outlined box holds a class from one of the schools, which consists of 15 to 30 children. Then, we add various colored lines as tracks, starting offstage and leading to the boxes. The dancers line up in the wings, hallways, and various holding areas on either side of the stage. At the end of the overture, they burst onto the stage, running and leaping and following their colored tracks to their respective boxes, where they explode into the opening dance number.

We had less than three minutes to accomplish "the runs." It's as if a couple of dozen trains coming from different places and traveling on different tracks all arrived at a station at the same time, safely pulling into their allotted spaces. But even before starting, it would take us almost an hour just to get the dancers lined up in the correct holding areas offstage, ready to make their entrance. We had scheduled one shot to rehearse the opening. It had to work the first time, or we would have to repeat everything. That would mean going into overtime at a great expense.

I gave the cue to start the number. The orchestra, singers, lights, and stagehands all commenced on cue, and the avalanche of 2,000 children was let loose on their tracks. "The runs" had begun!

After about a minute, I realized something was wrong. There was a big pileup on stage left, and children were colliding into each other and bunching up behind some obstacle. I ran over to discover the source of the problem: Michael and his classmates. He had ignored everything and led the group from his school right up front, as close to the audience as he could get. Inspiring his dancing buddies, they were a crew of leaping, contorting demons—dancing up a storm, but blocking some 600 other dancers trying to get through.

I rushed up to them, yelling, "You're in the wrong place! Back up! Back up!"

Michael—with his eyes blazing, mouth open, and legs and arms spinning in dance movements like an eggbeater—yelled out, "Oh, I am so happy! I am so happy! Thank you, Jacques! Oh, it's so good! I am so happy!"

I backed off, stunned into silence. I sat down in the first row of the audience and was joined by several of the supervisors, teachers, and chaperones from Michael's school, our mouths open in wonder. The spirit of dance had taken over Michael and his classmates. No one danced better or with more passion in the whole show that night and with Michael leading the way—the JOY OF DANCE was at work. (We went into overtime, but so what!)

—Jacques D'Amboise
Author of *Teaching the Magic of Dance*, winner of an
Academy Award for *He Makes Me Feel Like Dancin'*,
and Founder of the National Dance Institute

Middle Eastern Dance Comes to America

Solomon Bloom attended school for only one day because his parents could not afford to buy him books. The son of Polish immigrants, he was subsequently educated at home by his mother in San Francisco, where he also began working in a brush factory at the age of seven. By the age of 16, he had established a business of his own and was already wealthy. He was a regular visitor to Woodward's Gardens, San Francisco's first museum, which he considered a valuable source of instruction. Bloom produced a play and even built his own theater by the time he was 17 years old.

At the age of 19, "Sol" Bloom decided to tour the world to further his education, and his first stop was the 1889 Paris Exposition Universelle. On the exposition grounds, he saw incredible exhibits from throughout the world that showcased the wonders of science, industry, art, history, anthropology, and culture. The one exhibit that really captured his imagination was that of an Algerian village. Although he was intrigued by all that he saw, it was the women's traditional dancing that fascinated him most. He was not quite sure how he would showcase the dance troupe, but he felt certain that if he could bring them—or even the entire exhibit—to the United States, he could make a fortune with it. Bloom negotiated with their manger and, for a fee of about $1,000, obtained the right to negotiate a contract to exhibit them in North and South America.

Shortly after his return to the United States, Bloom learned of plans for the World's Columbian Exposition, or World's Fair, which would commemorate the four hundredth anniversary of Columbus's arrival in the New World. The chief contender to host the large international fair was the city of Chicago. It was awarded the international exhibition rights in 1890, when President Benjamin Harrison signed the exposition bill into law. Early in their planning, the commissioners offered the ambitious 21-year-old the position of manager of the Midway Plaisance, the area that contained all the amusement concessions of the fair. When asked to name the salary that he required, Bloom knew that he had a lot to consider and asked for one night to think about it. When he seriously reflected upon the offer, he realized that if he accepted the job, he would have to relocate to Chicago, leaving his family and home as well as his successful San Francisco businesses in the hands of others.

The following day, fully expecting to be refused, he asked for $1,000 per week. Much to his amazement, the agent for the commissioners agreed. Just a few months earlier, his greatest ambition had been to contract a spot on the Midway. Now he would be managing it—and at a salary that equaled that of the president of the United States!—all at the tender age of 21.

THE MIDWAY PLAISANCE

In the days before television, events such as these international expositions brought millions of people together in an important new way of sharing and exchanging ideas and experiences. Historians agree that the Chicago fair changed the world in many ways. The architecture of the Columbian Exposition was spectacular, and the whitewashed exteriors of all the buildings caused some to name them the "White City." Japan's pavilions introduced its traditional style of architecture to the Midwest, which later influenced the great American architect Frank Lloyd Wright.

Other important seeds of change were sown at the exposition as well. Milton S. Hershey purchased an entire chocolate-making assembly

This painting of the World's Columbian Exposition by T. de Thulstrup shows the main thoroughfare, called Midway Plaisance, at the 1893 Chicago World's Fair. On the right is the Dahomey Village, while the Austrian Village is behind it. The dome of the Moorish Palace can be seen in the far distance.

line he saw displayed there, enabling him to mass-produce the first affordable chocolate bars. Musicians from the South introduced the world to the catchy new rhythms that would eventually become known as ragtime. The first motion pictures and even the invention of the zipper have been associated with the fair. It was also there that a shocked America first encountered what would become known as the *hootchy-kootchy* dance.

About 200 separate buildings were constructed for the fair, with exhibitions about agriculture, electricity, fisheries, forestry, machinery, manufacturing, liberal arts, mines, stocks, and women. Every state and territory of the Union and 19 foreign countries constructed buildings of their own. There were also formal discussions of medicine, education, finance, religion, evolution, and art. When planners decided upon a separate amusement and exhibition area, they had expected that this area would pay for the huge expenses of the event and make the fair more popular with working-class people.

The Midway Plaisance was built on a strip of land 600 feet wide and almost a mile long. Under the direction of Harvard professor F.W. Putnam and the exposition's Department of Ethnology, the exhibits in that area were supposed to be collected from regions throughout the world and to show the progress and development of human civilization. This was to be achieved by building models of working villages complete with natives of the countries they were meant to represent. Sol Bloom was brought in by the commissioners to work on creating an impressive show that would draw crowds and make money.

In the first few months, ticket sales to the World's Fair were disappointing. The national economy was faltering, and a number of banks had failed. It was thought that the cold spring weather, expensive railroad fares to Chicago, and the harvest (which prevented rural folk from traveling until after its conclusion) were all adverse factors. There was also some controversy about the fair being open on Sundays, but in the end, it was generally accepted that it was the only day the majority of the working class could attend.

The most bold and daring visitors could see the fair in its entirety from high above the ground in the balloon ride, but the most otherworldly area was the Midway Plaisance. The foreign world created by the international concessions included villages representing Algeria, Turkey, Java, Germany, Austria, Ireland, and Lapland. An Egyptian street in Cairo (usually referred to simply as Cairo Street), a Hungarian Orpheum (restaurant and music hall), a Dahomeyan settlement, an Eskimo camp, a Chinese joss house, a Samoan settlement, and a group of Jahore bungalows rounded out the view of the world available to fairgoers. With so much to see, it probably would have taken weeks and much walking to view everything, but it seems that one exhibit attracted more visitors than any other.

CAIRO STREET

Attracting more than 2 million visitors in six months' time, Cairo Street was a model of how the people of Cairo lived, transacted business, and amused themselves. In addition to a replica of the Luxor Temple and a mosque, there were more than 60 shops. In the Cairo Street Theatre, performers usually called "dancing girls" had their performances labeled by a number of names, most notably *danse du ventre*—French for "dance of the stomach."

There were at least 12 female dancers who accompanied themselves with tiny cymbals attached to their fingers. They were joined by male musicians who played traditional instruments, including reed flutes, oud (the original lute), and a variety of percussion instruments. The Algerian, Tunisian, and Turkish villages also gave performances that were intended to be authentic portrayals of music and dance from their respective countries, even though they were performed on Western stages. Sadly, this was not the case everywhere on the Midway, and these performances contrasted sharply with those at the Persian Palace.

Just before the official opening of the exposition, Sol Bloom escorted his dancers to a press conference where they were to give reporters a preview of their art. Their costumes and appearance must have intrigued the men as Bloom introduced them. Rather than have them dance accompanied by their fellow countrymen on traditional instruments, as they were accustomed to doing, Bloom personally sat down at the piano. Using only one finger, he improvised what he imagined to be a Middle Eastern tune. Bloom's melody may well have been based upon one that was authentic, and there is some evidence that suggests that it was the familiar tune that has come to be identified with hootchy-kootchy, or belly dance. It has endured for more than 100 years, and is still frequently used in cartoons, television, and movies to support many exotic themes, including snake charmers.

By presenting the dancers in this manner, Sol Bloom joined the company of many artists and writers of his day whose work reflected what they imagined (and wished) Eastern culture to be—rather than what it really was. Known as the Orientalists, painters such as Eugène Delacroix, Jean-Léon Gérôme, and Gustave Moreau, and writers such as Lord Byron, Gustave Flaubert, and Victor Hugo were among those who contributed to this style of art and literature. Artists who felt disappointed when the appearance of real Middle Eastern women was not what they had imagined frequently chose beautiful Caucasian women dressed in fantasy versions of Arabic clothing to pose for their Oriental paintings and photographs, thereby perpetuating the myths.

Many Western artists, such as Eugène Delacroix, depicted the Middle East in a romantic—and often inaccurate—way in their paintings. Images of Middle Eastern women, such as those in Delacroix's *The Women of Algiers in Their Apartment (above)*, were often embellished and made to look Caucasian by Western artists.

THE PERSIAN PALACE

An impressive structure with towering minarets and domes, the Persian Palace of Eros originally included a company of Persian men who displayed athletic skills, gem cutting, carpet weaving, and other traditions of their country. Some of the male athletes with huge clubs performed demonstrations to the music of flute and drum, but this entertainment failed to excite fairgoers, so the management decided to change the program. They hired a troupe of female dancers from Paris to perform Faux-Oriental dance in skimpy costumes for male audiences. Not surprisingly, the French dancers attracted huge crowds, and a grossly distorted picture of Persian dance was presented to the masses.

Though the Midway Plaisance was an amazing spectacle in its own right, the public sadly seemed to have preferred the Orientalist fantasies to the real thing. This was hardly surprising, though, because in spite of a few reformers' lofty speeches about uplifting humanity, the villagers were generally looked upon as inferior. Nonwhite Americans were not included in planning the fair, though one day was observed for people of color. Native Americans were portrayed as savages, and the few people who tried to object were ignored.

As soon as Chicago's 1893 fair closed, amusement parks, carnivals, and circuses began to cash in on the popularity of the Middle Eastern entertainment from the Midway Plaisance. Since the French dancers in fantasy costumes had been so successful during the fair at the Persian Palace, it was not surprising that other non–Middle Eastern women were brought in to perform the danse du ventre, which was now nearly always referred to as the hootchy-cootchy. Oriental sideshows were also featured in the later international expositions in San Francisco, Atlanta, Nashville, Buffalo, and St. Louis.

These new dancing girls commonly used stage names, and regardless of the performers' real nationalities, their names usually evoked the Middle East. The most popular name was Little Egypt, and at one point, there were so many entertainers using that name that it became synonymous with that type of performance. Many old photographs of sideshow dancers still exist, some of them with costumes and poses that look genuine, and just as many that are obviously not. A performer known as Madame Ruth was featured in the 1894 kinetograph *Dance du Ventre*. A surviving film of a truly authentic-looking performance from around 1897 at Coney Island, New York, is entitled *Fatima's Dance*.

One of the more interesting places claiming to have employed the talents of Little Egypt is a popular tourist site called the Birdcage Theater. Located in the infamous Arizona Territory town of Tombstone, a bullet-scarred oil painting of an Oriental dancer still hangs above the bar of the former outlaw hangout. A plaque at the bottom of the portrait names the subject as Fatima, later known as Little Egypt, who played the Birdcage in 1881—12 years prior to the Chicago World's Fair. If that information is accurate, Fatima may well have been the first belly dancer to perform in the United States.

The incident that really brought the Little Egypt persona to the attention of the public was a scandal that has come to be known as the "Awful Seeley Dinner." A grandson of the famous circus showman

P.T. Barnum gave a bachelor party for his brother in a fashionable New York City restaurant. Captain George S. Chapman turned up to investigate a tip that indecent dancing was the planned entertainment. Although the dancer—who called herself "Little Egypt"—was hidden away until the policeman had left, and no arrests were made that night, reporters jumped on the story, as this was quite scandalous in 1906. In the ensuing investigation, the captain, Little Egypt, and many others were required to testify before the police board. Although several indictments were handed down, the charges were all dropped several months later.

When the scandal broke, Oscar Hammerstein—the Broadway producer and grandfather of one-half of the famous Broadway writing team of Rodgers and Hammerstein—took advantage of the publicity and created a burlesque spectacle called *Silly's Dinner*. It ran for two months at the Olympia Theatre at 44th and Broadway and starred the same Little Egypt and other entertainers who had appeared at the real dinner. That was the first time a current event became the basis for a show in a music hall. However, though the newspapers extensively reported both the Awful Seeley Dinner and the *Silly's Dinner* comedy, none of those reports suggested that Little Egypt had danced at the Midway Plaisance. That is probably because the young woman who performed at both the infamous bachelor party and at the Olympia Theater was a petite Algerian named Ashea Wabe, and there is no evidence that Wabe had anything to do with the World's Fair.

Farida Mahzar probably did dance at the fair. Although the details of her life and career are shrouded in mystery, it is believed that she was Syrian and that she had learned to dance in Cairo, Egypt. It is generally accepted that she performed on the Midway Plaisance and was part of the surrounding controversy, but she eventually married a Greek restaurateur and became a devoted wife. Mahzar continued performing occasionally, but in a conservative manner unlike that of her many imitators. Shortly before her death, she sued the makers of the 1936 motion picture *The Great Ziegfeld* because they presented Little Egypt as a lewd character. Fourteen different witnesses gave depositions that they had seen her perform at the 1893 Chicago World's Fair, all swearing that her performances were skilled and never lewd, and that her midsection had never been seen uncovered. Farida Mahzar died of a heart attack before her lawsuit came to trial, and her obituary noted that she claimed to be the original Little Egypt.

According to popular legend, the famous author Mark Twain suffered a coronary upon seeing her dance, and Thomas Edison's film of her performance caused the motion picture camera to become an instant success. It is highly doubtful that either story is true. It is possible that the dancing of someone else who used the name Little Egypt may have caused Twain to have a heart attack. It could not have been Mahzar, though, because Twain was ill while he was in Chicago and never set foot on the fairgrounds. As for Edison, he had intended to display his new motion picture camera, the kinetoscope, but technical difficulties kept him from completing it in time for the exhibition. If the famous inventor had made a moving picture of one of the infamous dancers at the fair, it would almost certainly have been front-page news.

Probably the strangest thing attributed to Little Egypt was that she helped launch the invention of the zipper. It has been said that it enabled her to change costumes more quickly during her performances in Chicago. Others claimed that the newly invented electric Ferris wheel and the sideshow featuring the belly dancer Little Egypt caused the world's first zipper to be ignored.

It should be remembered that in the late nineteenth century, American women were still tightly laced into corsets, and the sight of a female ankle (even in thick stockings) was considered risqué. Any woman who performed in public was automatically assumed to be of low moral character. It is hardly surprising that the costumes and movements of the female dancers who entertained fairgoers caused quite a stir. In spite of the controversy, Cairo Street was indisputably the most awe-inspiring spectacle there. Crowds enjoyed the fortune-telling, camel and donkey rides, and snake charmers, but it was definitely the dancing girls that intrigued the public most of all. It seems that they equally repulsed and fascinated fairgoers.

By 1948, Sol Bloom had become a member of Congress and chairman of the House Committee on Foreign Affairs. Congressman Bloom was considered an authority on amusements at the fair, yet he denied that there was ever a dancer called Little Egypt on the Midway. He further added that there was a riding camel by that name in Cairo Street. Some think that perhaps he was embarrassed to admit to ever having known a performer of such notoriety. Others who knew him well felt sure that he would have enjoyed claiming the acquaintance of the real "Little Egypt."

Sol Bloom (*left, with fellow congressman Charles Eaton*) is pictured shortly after becoming chairman of the House Committee on Foreign Affairs in 1948. Bloom denied that there ever was a performer named Little Egypt at the 1893 Chicago World's Fair.

There is no conclusive evidence regarding who the original Little Egypt really was, or even when or where she first appeared, even though many different women have claimed that title during the past 100 years. However, it seems clear that all the documented references to her as a specific dancer at the 1893 exposition were written long after the event. The hard evidence that has survived in the form of photographs, playbills, advertisements, and even farewell poems to the Midway dancers published in the local newspapers and other forms of memorabilia never mention her. Although many photos of dancing girls from the fair have survived, not a single one is verifiable as Little Egypt.

In spite of the lack of historical evidence, many still stubbornly cling to the belief that Little Egypt of Columbian Exposition fame was America's first notable belly dancer. She lives on in our history, reference, and dance books, and has become a popular legend. Her true identity, her dance, and even whether she ever existed remain a mystery.

THE REAL MIDDLE EAST

The Middle East has often been called the Cradle of Civilization. The birthplace of Judaism, Christianity, and Islam, it is an area whose influence has also deeply impacted the disciplines of science, medicine, architecture, and certainly music and dance. Though there were a few bold travelers to the region as early as the Middle Ages, and later occupations by colonial armies, it was not until the nineteenth century that the Middle East (often called the Orient) became a fashionable destination for wealthy travelers. Among the curiosity-seeking Europeans, word quickly spread that the dancers were one of the region's most interesting attractions. Writers and painters flocked to the Middle East and North Africa for inspiration. For their part, some of the more enterprising people of the East soon learned that their foreign visitors provided a lucrative new market for their talents, and thus began the West's love-hate relationship with Middle Eastern dance. Throughout its long history, it has continued to fascinate and, at the same time, appall audiences everywhere it has been seen.

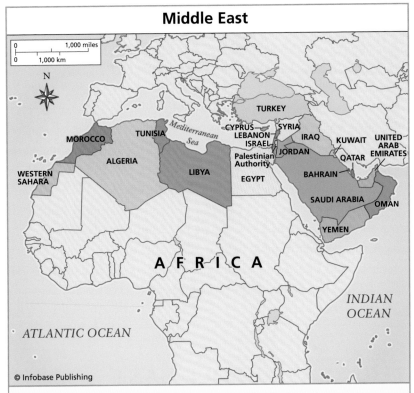

Middle East

Known as the Cradle of Civilization, the Middle East has always fascinated Westerners. Though it has no clearly defined boundaries, the region is loosely defined as stretching from Morocco in the west to Iran in the east and Turkey in the north to Yemen in the south.

Since the nineteenth century, many folk dance forms have become less popular in their homelands due to a number of factors, including governmental policies and interference, as well as the increasing influence and outright oppression by conservative elements and fundamentalist religious sects. In the best of circumstances, genuine ethnic/historical dance is not easily documented, but due in part to the growing Western interest, many important Middle Eastern dances have been documented and recorded before they were entirely extinguished.

Sadly, many customs and traditions of that vast and diversified part of the world are viewed and judged with as little understanding or appreciation of their ancient roots today as they were in the past. In recent years, as political tensions and turmoil have increased, the cultures of the East and West have collided in new ways, due in part to the West's dependence on the oil supplies of the East.

Though it still receives mixed reviews, despite all the odds, Middle Eastern dance has survived for thousands of years. The mysterious art, with its many and varied forms, has crossed the seas and found acceptance and appreciation in many countries around the world. It is a creative and unifying force among people wherever it is practiced.

North African Dances

THE OULED NAÏL

The Ouled Naïl (pronounced OO-led nile) are a prosperous people from the desert and mountain regions of Algeria. Through paintings of the Orientalists and later through photographs of the tribes' elaborately dressed dancers, Algeria provided familiar images of the exotic East to the Western world in the nineteenth century. The first Ouled Naïl dancers to perform in the United States arrived in 1893 as part of the group of Middle Eastern entertainers that Sol Bloom imported for the Chicago World's Fair.

When they were very young, the girls of the tribe began training not only in dance, but also in the art of pleasing men. Traditionally, they left their desert towns and villages for larger cities where they began to practice their trade when they were as young as 12. They would spend as long as 15 years working there, earning money until they finally returned to their desert homes to marry, using their savings as a dowry. How well they married generally depended upon how much money they had been able to save, but once they retired and married, they became good wives and mothers.

Residents of the desert and mountain regions of Algeria, the Ouled Naïl, are known for their belly dancing. From an early age, young girls of the tribe leave their villages to earn money by dancing in larger towns and cities. Pictured here is an Ouled Naïl woman in Algiers circa 1900.

Historically, dancers who perform publicly have been looked upon with suspicion and disapproval in the Middle East and generally have been assumed to be disreputable. The dancing women of the Ouled Naïl, however, have always been valued by their own tribes, and their ability to earn money both accepted and condoned. After their retirement, not only the dancers themselves but also their husbands and families are given great respect and can always take pride in their accomplishments and success.

Even at a time when almost all other women in North Africa were veiled, the dancers of the Ouled Naïl were not. They wore heavy black eye makeup and practiced facial tattooing. Their oiled, black hair was worn in looped-up braids and then covered with decorated veils. They dressed in long, full skirts and shawls with very elaborate headdresses and wore a tremendous amount of jewelry (made of real silver and gold), including bracelets, earrings, and necklaces. One of the most interesting types of jewelry worn by the girls was a large bracelet with long, sharp studs and spikes that protected them from unwanted attention from men. (Sadly, this protection was sometimes insufficient, because many of the girls were attacked and even murdered by would-be suitors, and their hard-earned wealth was stolen from them.)

They also wore the money they had earned as decoration and as tangible proof of their personal wealth and success at their trade. This display sometimes took the form of long necklaces made of coins, or coins fastened directly to their clothing or decorating their headdresses.

The costumes have evolved somewhat, and although they still have the same general look, the rich natural fabrics and real silver and gold coins of yesteryear are rarely seen today. Much of the material used in making the costumes is synthetic, and some dancers completely cover their faces with a transparent veil. Those who are able to sing as well as dance are able to earn more money and can generally work to ages older than they did in the past.

The dance style is heavy and earthy. In times past, some dancers would first perform in their traditional costumes and, upon request, later go behind a screen and remove most of their costumes, return, and continue to dance, wearing only the headdress and jewelry. The twisting hip movements common to many North African dances were accompanied by shoulder shimmies, strong muscular movements of the belly, and snakelike arm movements.

A famous American dancer named Ted Shawn (husband of the legendary dancer Ruth St. Denis) saw the Ouled Naïl dancers in the early 1900s and found them disgusting. Being a typical white tourist of the day, he was probably offended by their appearance and body language, and would likely have disapproved of them morally as well. However, many other witnesses of the time admitted to amazement and even grudging admiration for the mastery these women demonstrated over parts of the body for which most people have no control.

Although there are still some young women who follow this historical practice of their tribes, it is not as common as it once was; the increase in Islamic fundamentalism has no doubt caused it to be viewed in an extremely unfavorable light. Bou Saada is home to the best-known troupe of contemporary musicians and dancers, and tourists still sometimes visit that area of Algeria. A performance is typically done to live music, and soloists and groups are alternated.

The men of the tribe also perform and are well known for a dance incorporating their rifles. They typically wrap part of their head to veil the lower portion of their faces, especially their mouths. Many varieties of images document performances of this type, frequently accompanied by demonstrations of their famous skill in horseback riding. Most performances now begin with a procession led by the musicians with all participants clapping, shouting, and engaged in general merrymaking.

From time to time, tribes continue to gather and set up their tents for festivals and holidays when the Ouled Naïl entertain informally for those who attend. Contemporary women's performances are probably more similar to the typical belly dance in appearance than that of the traditional dance of yesteryear. The purpose of the dance performances is still to attract potential patrons for the dancers. In the past, some towns became famous because of the presence of Ouled Naïl dancers and are notorious for that reason today.

THE GHAWAZEE

It is believed that Gypsy tribes moved into the Middle East—probably from northern India—as early as the fifth century A.D. Many of them became traveling entertainers. Although it was their habit to adopt (at least on a superficial level) the religion of their host countries, they were still considered to be outsiders. Therefore, even after the advent of Islam, they were not subject to the same restrictions as the local Islamic population.

Those who settled in Egypt came to be known as the Ghawazee. Unlike most other Middle Eastern peoples, the Ghawazee traditionally preferred female babies over male, probably because of their ability to earn money. Traveling from city to city, the women danced in the streets, solo or in small groups, while the men accompanied them on instruments.

Although it is well documented in tomb paintings that professional dancers have worked in Egypt since Pharaonic times, dancing was neither an important nor respectable profession. The few elite Egyptians who were able to write kept no written record of their dancers to describe what they wore, what they were called, or what their dances were like. Therefore, the earliest known descriptions of Egyptian dancers were written by Europeans who were traveling in the Middle East as early as the 1600s.

When Napoleon led the first organized expedition to Egypt in 1798, he was trying to find an alternate route to India. He was accompanied by scholars who produced excellent documents recording what they learned about the country. There were many entertainers who lived in Cairo and along the banks of the Nile, and it was there that the French soldiers first saw the Ghawazee (meaning "thieves of the heart"), the Gypsy dancers of Egypt.

Although they were popular with the soldiers, the generals disapproved of them, and under the orders of one of Napoleon's generals, 400 of the Ghawazee were captured, beheaded, and thrown into the Nile in sacks. The French officials then forced those who remained to live together in houses for the convenience and comfort of their soldiers. The dancers were forced to be checked regularly by doctors and also to pay taxes on their earnings.

By the late nineteenth century, Egypt had become a common part of the fashionable "Grand Tour" of Europe often taken by wealthy people from Western countries. A few of those early travelers made a real effort to understand the native people and their culture and customs. Most of them, however, preferred to believe the fantasy of the decadent exotic

As evidenced by these tomb reliefs in Saqqara, Egypt, dance has been an important part of Egyptian culture for millennia. However, it did not become well documented in Egypt until Europeans came to the region in the 1600s.

world of the East that was such a stark contrast to their own very restricted Victorian societies.

Early pictures of the Ghawazee women show them wearing low-cut, fitted vests or longer tunics, usually with sleeves fitted to the elbow, which then hung loose from the elbow down. They often wore fairly sheer blouses underneath and either very full pants that fit at the ankle (often called harem pants) or full skirts underneath. A scarf tied around the hips was a standard item. The Gypsy women in Eastern Europe were wearing very similar clothing at the time. In contrast to the often revealing costumes of delicate, gauzy materials worn by most belly dancers even today, the Ghawazee costumes were usually made of heavier fabrics and did not allow as much freedom of movement. Both men and women blackened the rims of their eyes with kohl and used henna on their hands and feet, much like other Egyptians of the middle and upper classes.

The main movement of the dance of the Ghawazee has been described as a rapid vibrating, or shimmying, side-to-side motion of the hips performed to very fast music. (While hip shimmies are common to many Middle Eastern dances, they are more typically a vertical up/down hip movement, rather than twisted forward and backward.) They also incorporated back bends and sometimes floor work and head slides into their performance. The use of finger cymbals seems to have been a standard feature of the dance. The dancers also sang, told jokes, and engaged in light banter with their audience.

The Ghawazee danced to traditional folk music that had a distinctive and primitive sound. The instruments used include the *mizmar* (similar to a very loud oboe) and *tabla beledi* (simple drum), and sometimes also the *rebaba* (the one-stringed predecessor of the violin). The rhythm commonly associated with the Ghawazee is often simply called "Beledi," and its sound is approximated by the following syllables: DUM DUM ticky tack DUM ticky tack ticky DUM DUM ticky tack DUM ticky tack ticky, and so forth.

Much of the character of belly dancing as we know it today has probably come to us from the Ghawazee. The Mazin family of Luxor, Egypt, is recognized to be the Ghawazee's legitimate descendants. Known as *Banat Mazin* ("the daughters of Mazin"), they call their dance *raqs sha'abi,* meaning "folk dance," as opposed to the more familiar *raqs sharqi,* which translates to "dance of the East/Orient," but is widely understood to mean belly dancing. However, it has often been observed that belly dancers move around more than the Ghawazee, using a greater variety of movements (particularly of the arms), and that they perform to a more varied and classical form of Middle Eastern music.

Today, the custom of hiring the descendents of the Ghawazee to dance at weddings and other village celebrations is fading away due to a number of factors, Islamic fundamentalism and its disapproval of such entertainments chief among them. Fortunately, one member of the Mazin family still performs occasionally and, in recent years, has begun teaching privately. She even allows students to videotape, photograph, and record her performance, thus ensuring that there are accurate records of her ancient style of dance.

SAIDI

Many styles of popular Egyptian folk dance are loosely labeled "Saidi" (sigh-EE-dee) dance because they come from southern Egypt, which is also called Upper Egypt or simply the "Said" (sigh-EED). One of the best types of Saidi dance is known as *tahtib*, and paintings on monuments and tombs in the beautiful old city of Luxor document its ancient origins.

A battle dance that includes some of the thrusting and swinging movements of real combat, tahtib demonstrates skill with the thick, solid bamboo staff that Saidi men originally carried and used for herding, walking, and protection. The stick, usually seen as a prop in dance performances, is approximately 4 feet (1 m) long, but the original was used from horseback and was closer to 12 feet (3.5 m) long.

Tahtib is extremely masculine and dramatic and has the high energy shared by most Saidi dances. It is sometimes performed by a fairly large group, but they usually divide into pairs for the combat movements that

The region of Said, or Upper Egypt, has produced many styles of folk dance. Here, a woman in Luxor dances to the accompaniment of a variety of wind instruments while she plays the *sagat*, or finger cymbals.

are integral to the dance form. The men circle one another in search of an opening for attack while maintaining defensive postures and frequently exchange mock blows. To create the look of battle fought from horseback, one common step gives the dancer the characteristic bobbing motion seen when a man rides and is even called "the horse." There is much strutting and posturing as they show off their strength; they also feint, attack, and parry in time with the music.

Raqs assaya, the women's version of the tahtib, is softer and much more feminine and graceful. It utilizes smaller, lighter sticks that are often glitzy and colorful and can be either straight or hooked. Women handle their stick in a more delicate way, and often twirl their canes over their heads and off to the sides, sometimes lowering them, and then kicking them back up in the air. The canes are also balanced on the head and other parts of the body, and used to frame undulations and other more typical belly-dance-type movements. Some of the women's movements echo the tahtib, but they are not nearly as strong and militant in appearance.

Tahtib music is fairly primitive and features a double-sided bass drum called a *tavol*, which is worn strapped to the shoulders so that it hangs in front of the drummer. He uses the stick in his right hand to beat out the heavy "dooms" (rhythm like a heartbeat) and a lighter stick in the left hand to produce very quick "tahs." Most Saidi music is played on these traditional instruments and might also include the rebaba, the mizmar, and a flute with a shrill tone.

The standard dress of a Saidi man is a *galabiya* (GAL uh BAY uh). He'll sometimes wear two—one over the other and often in contrasting colors (one dark and one light). Yet another variation of the caftan-type garment that is so popular in hot desert countries, the Egyptian galabiyas are very loose and wide with round necks and loose sleeves. If only one is worn, a buttoned vest is usually worn underneath. A long strip of cloth is wrapped around the head into a fairly close-fitting turban with one end left hanging free. Another long, scarflike strip of cloth is worn loosely around the neck and tossed back over one shoulder. Most men also wear long, white cotton pants underneath and either short boots or sandals on their feet. All Saidi men wear mustaches as a point of masculine pride, and many of them protect their eyes from the harsh sun with kohl, as they have done since Pharaonic times.

Saidi women wear long, loose dresses (some with a ruffle around the hemline) and cover their hair with a scarf tied in the back, occasionally decorated with small, brightly colored pom-poms. For this and many other dances, shawls or scarves are tied around the hips; otherwise the movements of the body would be completely hidden in the fullness of the fabric. This style of dancing is done either barefoot or in flat slippers and should never be done in heels. Gold jewelry, including bangles on both arms, chandelier-type earrings, and heavy coin necklaces, are often worn by performers, but many older Saidi women actually wear very heavy-looking silver bangles (not fully enclosed) on their ankles.

3

Religious Dancing

THE WHIRLING DERVISHES

Known in the West as Whirling Dervishes, the men who try to connect with God through dance belong to an order that was founded by the Mevlana Jalaluddin Rumi (known to the English-speaking world as "Rumi"). Whirling (spinning in circles) is thought to have originated with central Asian shamans, or medicine men, who reached altered states of consciousness through its practice long before the time of Rumi. Dervishes are Sufis, and all Sufis are Muslims, but not all Muslims are Sufis.

Muslims believe that only one religion has truly ever been given, though it has been delivered by many messengers who have come to every group of people on Earth at some time in history. They believe that God is the source of all life and cannot be described or compared to anything but only known through the spiritual qualities that are manifest in the world and in the human heart. Islam considers itself the continuation of the Judeo-Christian tradition and accepts the Hebrew prophets, as well as Jesus and Mary. Muslims believe that attributing divinity to a human being is the primary error of Christianity. Muslims believe that Muhammad, the founder of their faith, is the last and greatest of

The whirling dervish is an example of religious ceremony transcending into performance art. Above, an entertainer performs a simplified version of the dance at the Al-Ghouri Mausoleum in Cairo, Egypt. Traditionally, the dance is performed by Sufi Muslims, who use the dance to show their devotion to God. When the whirling is a performance, rather than a religious ritual, the performer turns, or "whirls," endlessly while manipulating skirts in a colorful display, rather than following the exactly prescribed sequence of movements and ceremonial removal of cloaks, among other essential elements, of the authentic Sufi ceremonial ritual.

the human prophets who brought the message of God's love. By Rumi's time and in his world, Islam was well established. The average person performed regular *ablutions* (ritual washing) and prayed five times a day, fasted from food and drink during daylight hours for the month of Ramadan, and closely followed a code that emphasized the continual remembrance of God. Sufism is a mystical form of Islam with a central doctrine that promotes tolerance, piety, and love of God.

Mevlana Jalaluddin Rumi was born in 1207 in Balkh, which is part of Afghanistan today. In his mother tongue—Persian, the language of

Iran—*mevlâna* means "guide," and *rumi* means "from the Sultanate of Rum." Because of danger from Mongol invaders, Rumi's family eventually left Balkh and moved to Konya, Turkey, where his father, Bahauddin, became a prominent religious teacher at the university and also undertook his son's spiritual education. After his father died, Rumi's education was taken up by Seyyid Burhaneddin, one of his father's friends. Although he was still living in their old hometown of Balkh, Burhaneddin claimed to have sensed his friend's death, so he decided that he should move to Konya to take over the education of Rumi. For the next nine years, he tutored the young man in a wide variety of subjects, including religion, meditation, and fasting. During the same period, Rumi spent several years in Aleppo and Damascus studying with other great religious minds of the time.

Burhaneddin finally felt he had met his obligation and that he was free to retire and spend the rest of his own life in seclusion, because he had shared all of his knowledge with Rumi. Before going, he prophesied to Rumi that another great friend would come to him and that they would be like two halves of a whole, sharing the greatest friendship the world had ever known.

Highly educated by then, Rumi had become a religious leader and mystic with a following of his own. Then he met Mehmet Semseddin Tebrizi, also known as Shams, and just as Burhaneddin had predicted, the two men became great friends and companions. Under the influence of Shams, Rumi became a gifted poet, and his compositions were collected in a large volume called the *Divan-i Kabir*.

As close as the friends were, though, Shams vanished without explanation not once but twice. Sultan Veled, Rumi's son, searched for him and located him in Damascus after his first disappearance. The second time he was never found, and it is believed that he was probably killed by Rumi's own followers, who resented and feared his influence on their master. Rumi was so devastated by the loss of his friend that he withdrew from the world to meditate, and it was during that period that he wrote his greatest work, the *Mathnawi*.

Rumi also shared a deeply spiritual friendship with Husameddin Chelebi, who encouraged him to make a written record of his beautiful poetry. It is said that one day, with a smile, he pulled a scrap of writing containing the opening lines of his *Mathnawi* from the folds of his turban. It began by saying that one should listen to the "reed" (probably meaning a flute of some type), because it tells a tale and sings of separation. Chelebi is said to have wept for joy and begged him to continue with his writing. Rumi agreed that if his friend would be his scribe, he would recite for him. Sometimes the recitations came rapidly for days at a time, and other times they stopped completely for as long as two years. As each section was completed, Chelebi would read it back to the poet so that he could correct any mistakes.

Some say that the *Mathnawi* is the greatest spiritual masterpiece ever written by a single human being. It speaks about every aspect of life on Earth and discusses all human traits and character, as well as nature, history, and geography. It also addresses everyday life in both the physical and spiritual sense and is somewhat of a marvel because it is so complete.

Rumi died in December 1273. The brotherhood of Whirling Dervishes known as the Mevlevi was formally founded by his son. The dervishes were very influential during the Ottoman period, but Kamal Ataturk destroyed their orders early in the twentieth century and made museums of their monasteries. Many of the dervish orders continued to practice secretly until 1957, when they were again allowed to operate openly in order to preserve a historic tradition of Turkey.

Located in Konya, Turkey, the tomb where Rumi, his father, and his son are all buried is considered a shrine and visited by many pilgrims who come bearing food, gifts, and money. It is a tourist attraction to others and a fascinating part of Turkey's history. Konya is also the home of the country's largest festival. Culminating on December 17, the Mevlana Festival features performances of the whirling ceremony and celebrates the anniversary of Rumi's death, popularly referred to as the night of his wedding with Allah (the Arabic word for God).

Today, more than seven centuries after his death, poet and philosopher Rumi is recognized as a literary and spiritual figure of great importance by people of many different religions throughout the world. The order that has sprung from his practice and belief is unusual not only for its rites, but also for the freedom of thought (and fanaticism) it encourages within the framework of Islamic belief. This approach is focused upon spiritual love that is attained by a combination of music and dance through which the practitioner expresses devotion and attains ecstasy.

Turkey's largest festival takes place annually each December in the town of Konya. The Mevlana Festival features performances of the whirling ceremony (*pictured here*) and celebrates the anniversary of Mevlana Jalaluddin Rumi's death.

SUFISM

Most major religions have some members who believe that an emotional relationship with God is more important than following rules, and within Islam, those individuals are called Sufis. Their name comes from the Arabic word for rough, undyed wool (*suf*), because the early members of the order wore rough robes like Christian monks. Many of the earliest Sufis wandered from village to village living on charity; others were hermits. All of them rejected possessions and wealth as part of their search for a rich spiritual life and a close, loving relationship with God.

From roughly the twelfth to the nineteenth centuries, new Sufi orders continued to be established. Each order still has its own gathering place, called a *tekke*, and its own form of devotional and ritual practices to lead members into direct experience with the Beloved, who is God.

Eventually, some of the Sufi orders began to introduce saints and make shrines of their tombs. Mainstream Muslims felt that this was counter to the beliefs set forth by the Qur'an, which says that no prophet will come after Muhammad. Although it was considered the duty of a Muslim to marry and have children, some Sufis began to practice celibacy (refraining from any type of sexual activity) and engage in pagan customs such as glass eating and fire walking. There was also strong disapproval when they introduced music and a whirling dance to seek communion with God.

Sufism became widespread and popular in its many forms. Some recognized it as a legitimate outlet for religious fervor, but others were deeply concerned that Islam should be preserved and thought that the teachings of the Sufis deviated too far from the original form. The orthodox element quietly tried to solve the problem by taking control of the educational system throughout the Islamic world, thus ensuring that students would not be permitted to study subjects that might lead to confusion.

Nonetheless, Sufism played an important part in bringing Islam from the Middle East to other parts of the world, including India, Africa, and Southeast Asia. For example, it played a significant role in establishing Muslim political power in India to the extent that the Punjab remains a Muslim area to this day. Sufism appealed to Hindus and Buddhists who lived in the region because they already associated singing, dancing, and even whirling with attaining oneness with God. It also offered a new equality for the lower classes, which reduced some political tensions that existed there because of the caste system. That is why dervishes can still be found in many countries around the world, even though they are most closely associated with Turkey.

The whirling ritual, called *semâ*, is part of the Zikr ceremony. It begins with chanted prayers, followed by the beating of a kettledrum symbolizing the Divine order, after which a musical improvisation is played on a reed flute to represent the breath of life. The dervishes wear tall, cone-shaped hats made of felt to symbolize tombstones, and their long, full-skirted white robes represent their shrouds (burial clothes). They wear very full black cloaks over the robes to represent tombs. This costume is meant to show the death of their egos. The leader of the ceremony leads the dervishes around the perimeter of the room, and as they pass the main ceremonial position in the room, they bow to each other to show respect for the soul inside of each person.

Upon completion of three circles, the dervishes drop their black cloaks to show that they have given up their attachment to the world. Folding their arms across their chests, the dervishes approach the master one at a time, bow, kiss his hand, and begin to spin. Opening their arms wide, they raise their right arms and palms upward to receive blessings while their left palms and arms are held down to transfer that blessing to the earth. They always whirl counterclockwise (right to left, toward the heart). Eventually, all the dervishes are whirling at once until they slow down or stop as a group, kneel or pause slightly, and then rise to spin again for four repetitions. When they have completed the ritual, the leader reads a verse from the Qur'an reminding everyone that all directions belong to God, so wherever one turns, His face is there. The semâ is concluded by praying for the peace of the souls of all prophets and believers.

The whirling dancers of today are accompanied by poetry from the *Mathnawi* of Mevlana, set to traditional secular art music from the Ottoman period and sung. The musicians are usually trained professionals or composers who are part of the order, but they do not try to enter a trance state while making music. Traditional instruments used include the ney (flute), kanun (a plucked zither), kemenja (a lute played with a bow), tanbur (a plucked lute with frets), oud (fretless plucked lute), and kudum (pair of small kettledrums).

While authentic semâ still exists, the many imitations that are performed as secular entertainment today should never be confused with the devotional dancing of the Sufi mystics. Performed for tourists in many Middle Eastern countries, that type of dancing is an impressive display of balance and agility. For secular performances, the dancers wear one or more wide, brightly colored, gored skirts with weighted hemlines. When the dancers whirl, the skirts rise and undulate in a breathtaking kaleidoscope of movement and color. They sometimes separate the skirts, leaving one to whirl at the waistline while the other is lifted to spin in the air above the head, and sometimes further lifted to spin from one hand. Some performers also thrill their audiences further by including amazing manipulations of several tambourines in their acts. In Egypt, the secular form of the dance is called *raqs tanbur*.

The music of the dervishes is both beautiful and haunting, and recordings of it are readily available today, but it should be remembered that the chants are prayers. It would be absolutely inappropriate to use it for a belly dance performance of any kind. The music of the Sufis, like all sacred music, should be treated with respect.

GUEDRA

One of the most fascinating dances of the Middle East is a joyful kneeling trance dance called the *guedra*, which is attributed to the Blue People of the nomadic Tuareg Berber tribes of southwestern Morocco. They are

The Blue People of the nomadic Tuareg Berber tribes of North Africa are known for a number of traditional dances, including the *t'bal* and *guedra* (performed only by a female). Here, a Tuareg man performs a traditional dance as members of the tribe chant and clap their hands to the rhythm of the dance.

known as the Blue People because, as desert dwellers, they are unable to bathe regularly, and the powdered dye used for their shiny blue robes stains their skin and makes them appear blue. The blue tint serves as a cosmetic, as it is considered to be attractive, but the dye is also a natural moisturizer and sunscreen. All the Blue People belong to the Tuareg tribes, but there are other Tuaregs who do not wear these blue robes and therefore are not Blue People.

One of the most unusual features of the Blue People is the amount of power held by the females of the tribe. Unlike most Islamic societies, the women are unveiled, and the men cover their noses and mouths with the tail ends of their gauzy turbans, because it is believed that *djinn* (evil spirits) can invade the body through the mouth and nostrils. The women are not required to veil, because it is believed that they are divinely protected as life givers who are able to give birth to children.

A CEREMONY OF BLESSING

The guedra is a ritual dance that is meant either to deliver blessings and peace to others, such as friends, married people, or the community, or for the dancer to submit herself to God. Some even believe that the mystical drum rhythm can attract a mate from far away. A genuine guedra is usually danced by one woman at night by firelight or inside a tent with a circle of onlookers around her, but she is occasionally joined by others. Spectators are also participants as they chant and clap their hands to the hypnotic rhythm. One of the most unusual features of the dance is that it is normally performed entirely on the knees. If the dance is performed standing or even begun in a standing position, it is called *t'bal*.

Guedra means "pot" in Arabic, and the drum really is made from a common kitchen pot with goatskin stretched over its top. It is traditionally the only instrument used in the performance of this dance, and its beat mimics the heartbeat, the most basic rhythm of life (dah DAH dum dah DAH, dah DAH dum duh DAH), and gradually and steadily increases in speed throughout the dance.

Traditional clothing has always affected how people are able to move, so it has greatly influenced many ethnic dances. Most serious dancers make a great effort to emulate the look and feeling of authentic garments in their choice of costumes. Many Middle Eastern peoples have built their national dress around some type of flowing robe, and so have the Blue People. The women, like those in a number of other African cultures, wear an outer cloth wrapped around the body somewhat like an Indian sari. That cloth is held in place at the neck with elaborate fasteners and decorated with long chains. The waistline is belted so that the hem is just above the top of the foot. Leftover fabric is left flowing free but can be pulled up to cover the head if needed for protection from the weather.

The women wear elaborate, tall headdresses that are decorated with ornaments of silver, turquoise, coral, shells, and other items considered to look attractive. They also contain a wire frame that is held in place by the hair that is wrapped and woven over it. Not only does this look amazing, but it also keeps the women cooler in the heat and warmer in the cold. Constructing this remarkable hairdo is so time consuming and complicated that it is often left in place for a month or longer before being redone.

Some dancers begin completely covered by a black veil called a *haik*, and others are covered by the leftover blue fabric from their outer garments. This is meant to signify the darkness of the unknown.

The dancer's hands, decorated with henna, are seen first as they emerge shyly from the veil's sides, and she begins by saluting the four directions (north, south, east, and west) and the elements (earth, air, fire, and water). She gestures to her own abdomen, heart, and head and then flicks her fingers toward the spectators to bless them from the depth of her being. Since the rest of her body is still concealed, the movement of her hands takes on great importance. It is believed that the essence of the soul is exuded through a particular finger, so it is held separately from the others.

As the momentum of the drumming, clapping, and chanting builds, her breathing becomes heavier. She might walk or shuffle on her knees while keeping all movement above the waist still, especially in the fingers, hands, and arms. She continues undulating and leaning forward and into back bends until the haik falls away, and the dancer, eyes closed, becomes visible.

Movements of the head can be incorporated, and the rib cage can be lifted and dropped heavily in rhythm with the music for emphasis.

As the ritual increases in intensity, observers are drawn in so deeply that they begin to imitate the movements of the dancer, often not realizing that they are doing so.

Some dancers begin the dance with artificial braids and ornaments hidden in their hair or headpieces. Midway through the dance, they loosen them with a quick and subtle movement so that they hang free and swing to emphasize the swaying movements. The rhythm finally rises to a crescendo, and the audience becomes louder and even more enthusiastic. Then, in sudden silence, the dancer collapses to the ground in a faint, soon to be followed by another.

ZAR TRANCE

The *zar* is thought to be a kind of religious dancing that has its roots in the worship of pre-Islamic African deities, perhaps as a distant variation of what the West knows as voodoo. Because of its association with older pagan religions, it is prohibited by Islam. Most leaders and participants of the zar are women, though in some instances men have been permitted to help with drumming, the ritual slaughter of animals for sacrifice, or making offerings to the possessing spirit. Details of the ceremony vary widely from one area to another. Although the zar ceremony can be held publicly, it is often private and even conducted secretly.

Zar is especially prevalent in Upper (southern) Egypt, where the people have had less outside influence and are in closer proximity to the Sudan, Ethiopia, and Somalia, where it is more commonly practiced. Today, the zar is danced primarily for relaxation and spiritual healing. It is particularly popular with pregnant women who hope to ensure a safe birth. Some say that the ceremony is a kind of exorcism, while many others believe that it is a means of calming and satisfying the possessing spirit so that the person can live with it.

The ritual has a leader, or priestess, who could be called *hadjia*, *sheikha*, *umiya*, or a number of other names denoting respect depending upon the region. It was once believed that she was possessed by a spirit herself but was able to help others because she had learned to pacify or control her spirit. Older women have traditionally filled this role because unmarried younger females have not been considered worthy.

Zar musicians and healers perform their ritual in Cairo in June 2006. The Zar trans religious ceremony, which uses drumming and dancing to cure an illness thought to be caused by a demon, is performed across Egypt, though it is practiced as far south as Sudan. The ritual is prohibited by Islam as a pagan practice, but it continues to be part of Egypt's popular culture.

By singing directly to the inhabiting spirits and seeing which one reacts, the leader of the ceremony is able to identify the type of the troubling spirit and also understand how best to manage it.

(continues on page 52)

A'AZA: A RITUAL OF SUFFERING

During the time of the most recent war with Iraq, the Western world was confronted with images of chanting Shia Muslim men gathered in circles, rhythmically thrusting their arms into the air and then whipping them back with a loud, drumlike thump as the men slapped themselves across their chests in unison. Their faces were often highly charged with emotion based in religious fervor. Many of the men were obviously bruised and even bleeding, but though the ritual is violent in appearance, serious injury is unusual, and first aid is usually available nearby for all those who participate.

Although it may appear to be some sort of dance, *A'aza* is a ritual of suffering practiced solely by the Shia to honor the Imam Hussein, grandson of the Prophet Muhammad, who was martyred in the seventh century. He was killed and beheaded in a battle that occurred in the vicinity of Karbala, Iraq, because he refused to submit to the authority of the caliph Yazid. The presence of his tomb has made Karbala a holy city and the popular destination of Shia pilgrims. This ritual is also observed in connection with other Shia imams (there are 12 of them) and also in remembrance of the death of Fatima, the daughter of Muhammad.

The annual Shia pilgrimage to Karbala was still allowed during the time of the Sunni-dominated government of Saddam Hussein, but the public rituals involving chanting and flagellation were banned, as all gatherings that could potentially become large, emotional demonstrations were suppressed. However, those who wished to keep this tradition alive continued to practice it secretly.

A'aza is not performed alone, but in groups, ranging in number from just a few men to hundreds in one circle.

Each group has a leader, and the others follow the pace and rhythm he sets, until he eventually steps aside and another leader begins. Several circles can chant concurrently, and each group might have its own lyrics chanted in either a local dialect or in classical Arabic. Perhaps the most common one is "We will not forget." Most recently, some groups chanted about the fall of the regime and the hope of a new Iraq. The synchronization of the movement and the chanting is considered very important.

The Iraqi style is the most dominant form of the A'aza and is considered almost classical. However, several other regions take great pride in their distinctive local styles. In one style seen in Iraq, participants first strike their hearts with their right hands, then strike their chests with both hands, and finally strike their heads. There are a number of variations on this form, however, and a few are considerably more extreme. Some men beat their own backs with whips made of chains, cut their heads with long knives, and, in the act of *tatbeer*, strike their heads with swords.

There is controversy as to which elements of the practice are too extreme and about the exact form the chanting should take. Some Persian Gulf countries are more progressive than others, and periodically change the rhythm of the chants to create variety and a more musical sound. A few pioneers have even added music, and though very moderate sheikhs (holy men) accept that practice, there are others who object strongly.

Just a few men chanting slowly can begin the A'aza, but as the fervor builds, others usually join them. There is an element of friendly competition, and though most of the youngest participants admit that mature men are stronger and can make a louder slap or thump, they boast that the youths have more stamina. A procession often travels very

(continues)

(continued)

long distances in extreme heat and can last for days until it reaches the tomb of Hussein.

Although women do not participate in A'aza, they often watch from the side of the road and sometimes gently hit themselves or just tap their foreheads and cheeks in rhythm with the men. There are times, especially during the month of Muharrem, when women gather in a special house called the *Husseineya*, where they tell stories of the martyrs—even stories of Jesus that focus on how Mary suffered as a mother and a woman because of how her son was treated. Those rituals of mourning are also highly emotional and culminate in rhythmic jumping, hitting the chest, and chanting.

The ritual is especially associated with *Ashura*, which occurs on the tenth day of the month of Muharrem on the Islamic calendar. However, A'aza is not performed solely to mark religious occasions, but also used to show solidarity among the Shia about situations and events that impact the Islamic world, such as the plight of the Palestinian people and political upheaval and outside intervention in places such as Afghanistan, Kashmir, and lately Iraq.

(continued from page 49)

The zar is usually danced in an area containing an altar. This space is usually separate from the living quarters. A round tray piled with offerings of nuts and dried fruits is placed in the center of the room. The leader and her musicians are on one side of the room, and the participants fill the rest of the space. Everyone is expected to make a financial donation to the leader, and it is known that she will be willing to provide charity to women in the community when they have need. Animal sacrifice—ranging from a chicken or pigeon to a sheep or camel—was once a standard element of the zar but is no longer included in all ceremonies. Providing some kind of food and beverage as a shared meal for the participants usually concludes the ceremony.

The woman who is being treated frequently wears some sort of loose white clothing and decorates her hands with henna and lines her eyes with kohl, both materials that are believed to be blessed. These cosmetics along with perfumes or incense (*bokhur* in Arabic) are thought to please the spirits. It is not uncommon for the participants to change clothes to accommodate different spirits, and in some areas, red garments are preferred.

The percussion instruments used to provide rhythm could include a variation of the tambourine (*tar*) and a drum (*tabla*). The basic rhythm is very simple (DUM da-da DUM da, DUM da-da DUM da, etc.) beginning fairly slowly and gradually and steadily increasing in speed.

The opening movements can be just tiny, rhythmic jerks, though they vary widely as each woman responds to the music as she feels it. What is most commonly associated with the dance, however, is flinging the upper body—or only the head and hair—from side to side. Sometimes both arms are raised but kept relaxed so that they can rise and fall to follow the sway of the body in increasingly wild abandon until total collapse occurs.

The dance is still done in its original context but also as a performance that has the appearance of a real ceremony. As people in the West are becoming more interested in alternative methods of treating depression and illness, there is more experimentation with this and other types of "trance" dancing.

Dabkeh: Dance
of the Levant

Nearly all countries have traditional line and/or circle dances in which many people join hands and dance together all at one time in a uniform pattern of steps and figures. The Middle East is no exception, and one of its most popular and best-known dances is the *dabkeh* (DUB kee). It is a line dance associated particularly with the Levant, an old name for the region made up of Israel, Jordan, Lebanon, Palestine, and coastal Syria. Considered the national dance of Lebanon, it is also much beloved by Syrians, Jordanians, and Palestinians; it also is sometimes danced in Iraq. This dance is currently performed by many professional troupes at festivals and dance exhibitions, and by ordinary people of all ages at celebrations of all kinds.

Although at first glance it may appear to be rather monotonous and repetitive, on closer examination it is somewhat complex. It is exciting and fun for those who participate and is usually accompanied by much shouting and laughter. Amazingly energetic and tiring, the dance sometimes begins as a straight march and stamp, but it gradually becomes quite intricate and syncopated. Those who are adept at the dance slightly rock forward and back with the crossover steps, and rather than

Dabkeh is a popular social dance practiced throughout the Levant, the region composed of Israel, Jordan, Lebanon, the Palestinian Territories, and coastal areas of Syria. Here, Palestinian children dance the dabkeh in Gaza City in 2007.

punctuating the knee bends and kicks with a simple stamp, they beat out a quick rhythm with one foot to punctuate the figure.

The person who leads the dance, the *ras*, is usually the most talented, experienced dancer in the group. He or she is always at the right end (top) of the line and determines the pattern of the dance as he or she twirls a handkerchief or small scarf (over the head in the right hand) in time with the music. The ras begins by getting the line of dancers moving along well, and then he or she may break away from the line and demonstrate personal skill and style by adding leaps, quick turns, shoulder shimmies, more intricate footwork, and other embellishments. At this point, the ras might put hands on the hips, with elbows out. The ras sometimes moves up and down the semicircular line and challenges other dancers to join, match, or attempt to outdo his or her improvisation.

This dance can be done by men only, women only, or in mixed formation, all doing the same steps. The line, especially if it is long, may break off into smaller formations. Dancers usually join hands, and for some formations, the hands are clasped at hip level with the arms held ramrod straight, shoulder to shoulder, giving the dance a very interesting and distinctive appearance as they lean and sway their bodies in sync while performing uniform footwork.

HISTORY AND ORIGINS

The earliest form of the dabkeh may have been introduced by the Turks during the time of the Ottoman Empire when they ruled much of the Middle East. Certainly, the traditional costume favored by many professional performers is heavily influenced by nineteenth-century Turkish fashion, and Turkey has retained several folk dances that have a very similar appearance.

Historically, the dabkeh has played a significant role in village life, perhaps because it is a way of bonding a group of people together. According to folk tradition, stamping the feet on the ground also connects the people to their mother, the earth. This dance is currently performed by many professional troupes at festivals and dance exhibitions, and by ordinary people of all ages at most weddings, parties, and nightclubs where it often ends a happy evening. Dabkeh music has a distinctive sound, and as soon as it is heard, only one man or woman needs to start dancing before others will soon join.

Professional troupes often wear costumes that are similar or identical in design, but in different colors, patterns, or types of material to add visual interest. Others deliberately vary the designs to present the appearance of village folk. While the style of costume certainly varies from one place to another, it is based upon the native dress of the inhabitants. Each area might have certain features of the costume that would distinctively identify it as being from that particular place. If the dancing occurs at a wedding or party, as it so often does, the dancers could be wearing anything.

Men often wear full Turkish pants (tight at the ankle) with loose shirts, belted or sashed at the waists, and flat shoes or boots to emphasize the stamping steps. Women frequently wear peasant-style blouses with full skirts, sashes at the waist, and hip scarves. They sometimes wear headscarves (tied either behind the head or under the chin) and perhaps embroidered vests or jackets over the blouses. Alternately, women can wear belted tunics or overdresses, traditionally trimmed with heavy gold embroidery, with the aforementioned full Turkish pants sometimes worn underneath. Pillbox hats are also common, decorated with coins and veils that can either hang from the back or be draped under the chin and fastened on the other side.

There is a particular kind of music used for performing dabkeh. The most famous and popular female singer to come from Lebanon is probably Feyrouz, and several of her recordings contain good dabkeh music. "The Dal'ouna," "Aa Nadda," and "Al Houwara" are other Lebanese songs

For the people of the Levant, dabkeh is an integral part of their culture. Here, a professional troupe performs the dabkeh in the mountain village of Deir al-Qamar, southeast of Beirut, Lebanon.

that are synonymous with this dance. Traditional dabkeh music has six beats to the measure, but most modern pieces are written eight beats to the measure though they are still danced in six-beat patterns. (Modern pieces typically have fairly even rhythms, so this is not very difficult to do.) When there is live music, a person playing the *ney* (flute) sometimes participates in the dance while playing, and a very skilled drummer (*derbeki*) might also be able to combine dance while drumming. The much larger *tableh* drum is also frequently used.

The dabkeh symbolizes the will and strength of the people of the mountain villages who are accustomed to a tough way of life. It is enjoyed by everyone, and even those who are from the cities take pride in its performance. As often as they gather, the people of the Levant will be found dancing everywhere in the world, wherever they make their homes, in a continuing show of solidarity and love of their heritage.

Dances of the Arabian Gulf

A fascinating dance often seen by visitors to the Gulf is the ayyalah. The vision of rows of men uniformly swaying to a steady drumbeat in their white *thobes* has caused some to liken their appearance to the white crests of waves in the sea, which may have indeed been one of the influences on the development of the dance.

It is generally believed that traders from Upper Egypt (southern Egypt) and other parts of Africa came to the present-day United Arab Emirates in ancient times, bringing their music and dance with them. Over the passage of time, these dances have gradually changed, adapted, and finally become a cherished part of local tradition to be passed from one generation to the next.

The ayyalah is a battle dance performed with sticks by men ranging in age from the young to the very old. One person leads the singing, reciting tales of legendary bravery in battle and stirring strong feelings of love and patriotism in the dancers. The rhythm of drums remains steady and constant throughout, and against that backdrop, the voices continuously rise and fall, echoing the swaying movement of the rows of bodies. Even those who are unable to comprehend the language can nearly always understand and be moved by the feeling and the mood created when the ayyalah is performed.

Two long rows of dancers (at least 30 in each row, often many more) move forward and backward, in a mock battle, while each row sings challenges to the opposite side, bending forward and pointing the stick down to represent defeat, and bending back and pointing the stick skyward to signify victory. Occasionally, a third row of female dancers is present and attired in the traditional *thobe neshal* (described in the next section); they cheer the warriors by performing the famous *raqs nasha'at* (the Hair Dance).

The ayyalah is most often performed by professional dancers today and is only one in an extensive repertoire of dances from the region. Particular instruments, or combinations of instruments, are associated with each dance. Performers of ayyalah are accompanied by a very large bass drum (*al ras*) and three smaller drums called *takhmirs* as well as small cymbals and a tambourine.

Most of these men began dancing in childhood, learning from tribal elders or their own fathers. Those who showed the most talent eventually trained with teachers and finally formed their own professional groups. Some feel that because there are more distractions for modern youth, there is less enthusiasm for traditional dancing than in times past. Often with the support and encouragement of the government, many of today's professional dancers participate in educational projects to pass their art along to a new generation.

THE WOMEN'S "HAIR" DANCE

The Middle Eastern countries in the vicinity of the Persian Gulf and the Arabian Peninsula are collectively called the Gulf States and include Saudi Arabia, Kuwait, Bahrain, Qatar, the United Arab Emirates, Yemen, and Oman. (Some would include Iraq and Iran, although Iranians are Persians, not Arabs.) In Arabic, this area is called the *Khalij* (kha LEEJ), and the music, dance, and clothing from that area are all loosely referred to as *Khaliji* (kha LEEJ ee).

Perhaps because of the harshness of desert climates, many Middle Eastern people are inclined to nap and rest during the afternoon to

The women's hair dance is a popular form of cultural expression throughout the Persian Gulf region. Here, women swing their hair in rhythm to the music being played during a festival in Muscat, Oman.

escape temperatures that can be exceedingly high. As a result, they are even more inclined to entertain and socialize well into the wee hours of the morning when the weather is more pleasant. Extended family is extremely important in Gulf countries, and the women share warm, close relationships—perhaps even more so because many societies there continue to segregate men and women. Singing, dancing, and telling stories are ways that women strengthen those relationships and entertain themselves as well as preserve their rich heritage.

One of the notable dances of this area is the gentle, refined women's dance that, like other folk dances, is often seen at weddings and social functions that are celebratory in nature. It is known by a number of different names; for example, in Kuwait it is sometimes called *samra* or *samri*; in the United Arab Emirates it is known as *raqs nasha'at*; and to outsiders it is usually identified as Khaliji dance, Saudi dance, or *raqs na'shaar* ("dance of the hair").

The most famous and universally recognized movement of this dance is the hair being swung and tossed in time with the music. Although it has become fairly common for modern Arabic women to cut their hair, long hair has always been a symbol of female beauty in the Middle East and is still greatly admired. Those who are most revered are skilled dancers with hair that reaches at least to the waist, or even to the knees and below, who are able to send their tresses flying in breathtaking arcs, figure eights, and circles in perfect rhythm with the music. Certainly, the sight of rows of women with long hair performing this dance in their splendid costumes is an awe-inspiring and unforgettable spectacle.

One of the most striking features of *raqs nasha'at* is the garment associated with it, one that is worn for no other purpose. The thobe neshal is a very long, rectangular caftan-type garment that is usually made of brightly colored silky fabric. From the keyhole-shaped neck opening to the hem, a wide vertical panel runs all the way down the front of the dress. That panel, along with all the edges (sleeves, neckline, and hem) are heavily embroidered in gold or silver and often embellished with beads and sequins, a decoration that also adds considerable weight to the garment.

Because they are quite sheer as well as very long and loose, women bring their folded neshals with them in hand but do not wear them until they are going to dance. The neshals are pulled on over the head and worn right over the clothes. The enormous sleeves have huge arm openings both at the shoulder and the wrist, and one or both sleeves can be draped over the head to form a veil that also creates attractive folds.

The footwork is fairly simple, as the dancer takes small steps forward on the flat of one foot while staying on the ball of the other foot, which is locked into place just behind the flat foot that leads forward. This is done first with one foot leading, then reversed so that the opposite foot leads. It gives a sort of hopping or limping look as the dancers bob along together in time with the music. There are also steps that deliberately give a very smooth, gliding illusion, especially since the feet and legs are entirely hidden from view. Some of the motion of the dance originates from the shoulders and can range from relaxed accents alternating between the left and right shoulders to delicate shimmies.

Hip movements are very subtle and mirror the shoulder movements as the dancers move gracefully around the floor; no sort of hip scarf or belt is ever worn. The dancer holds much of her garment up with her hands; otherwise she would trip on it since the back of it trails onto the floor. The dancer manipulates the weighted fabric, often rhythmically swinging it from side to side.

The Khaliji music has a unique sound and is often known as Saudi music in Western countries. Women have their own variation of it. As most social gatherings in the Gulf States are still segregated, the women often have all-female bands to play at their parties, especially weddings. While the melodies are typically very simple, the percussion is rich, layered, and syncopated. Usually, the leader (*mutribah*) plays the oud and sings the main melody, and those who sing the chorus play several different percussion instruments, in varying pitches and rhythms. It is common for the audience to sing along, clap, shout encouragement, and, of course, engage in the ever-present ululation, the *zaghroota*. The women who provide music of this type are not generally judged by particular musical standards or criteria as they might be in Western countries, but rather by their ability to touch and move their audiences on an emotional level.

A live band is not always available, of course, so women also enjoy dancing to the recorded music of many popular Arabic singers. Though a number of songs are associated with the women's dance, the most famous one is entitled "Aba'ad" and usually called simply "Leila Leila." Written by a Kuwaiti composer (Yousif Mehana) and made popular by prominent Saudi singer Mohammed Abdou, it is almost synonymous with this dance throughout the Middle East.

AL ARDHAH

The music and dance of Saudi Arabia find their roots in the chants and melodies of poets and singing swordsmen of the country's ancient Bedouin past. Each region has its own style of music and dance, but the men's sword dance, *al Ardhah*, is probably the most familiar and is recognized both nationally and internationally in its association with Saudi Arabia. Considered the dance of the Najd, or central region of the vast

In Saudi Arabia, the men's sword dance, or al Ardhah, is one of the nation's most recognized dances. Here, Saudi King Abdullah bin Abdul Aziz (*center*) holds his sword during the al Ardhah at the Janadriyah Festival of Heritage and Culture, near Riyadh in 2007.

desert kingdom, it shares some features with the ayyalah of the United Arab Emirates in that it uses singers, dancers, and a narrator/poet. Long ago, it was a war dance, and women participated by holding swords to encourage the men to show their strength and courage in battle. Today, it is performed at important ceremonies, but women are no longer normally present either as spectators or participants.

Men carrying swords stand shoulder to shoulder in two long lines that face each other, normally toward the north and south. On the eastern and western sides, another two facing lines of men hold drums (*tubul*). At the center of one of the lines of swordsmen, one man holds a flag. Also positioned near the middle is the poet/narrator who begins by singing a verse or a short melody (*horabah*) to prepare the men for battle, and that verse is echoed by the chorus of men who repeat it. After several repetitions of the horabah, the drummers begin to beat out the slow, stately rhythm, and finally the dance begins, with the lines taking turns, advancing and retreating. The flagman accompanies the leader (usually a prince or other dignitary or guest of honor) forward to the middle of the square so that his dancing is showcased. The dance sometimes lasts for hours with each dancer having the opportunity to show his personal ability but all the while being part of the group.

Prominent members of the royal family of Saudi Arabia have regularly been seen joining the dance at important public events in the kingdom. In recent years, the current king (who was then Crown Prince Abdullah) and his brothers, Defense Minister Prince Sultan and Prince Abdul Majeed, the Governor of Medina, joined their countrymen in gesturing high with their flashing swords, much to the delight and enthusiastic applause of onlookers. Indeed, in 1931, wealthy and prominent Chicago philanthropist Charles R. Crane was the first American to officially visit the newly formed Kingdom of Saudi Arabia. He was intrigued when the son of King Abdul Aziz (often simply called Ibn Saud) performed in his honor.

6

Belly Dancing: The Evolution of the Woman's Solo

The dance most often associated with the Middle East is certainly that which is commonly referred to as the "belly dance," a name that conjures up images of dancers dressed in the costumes that most Americans and Europeans have always imagined to have been worn by the women of the harem. One of the more popular theories of the origins of that name is that upon seeing it for the first time, French soldiers who were stationed in North Africa—as long ago as the time of Napoleon—labeled it danse du ventre, meaning "dance of the stomach." Other sources credit the French name for the dance to Sol Bloom, and yet others claim it is a corruption of the Arabic word *beledi*, which generally refers to folk dance. In Arabic, it is never called belly dance, but rather *Raks Sharq'i*, which translates to "dance of the east." It is also known as *Raks Masri*—Egyptian Dance. Some call it *danse orientale*, which also means "dance of the East."

Belly dancing is probably one of the oldest surviving dances, and though its purest form may have been lost, it undoubtedly retains some

This romantic rendition of belly dance by Paul Louis Bouchard is typical of how many Westerners perceived *danse orientale* in the 1800s. Titled *Oriental Dancers* (*Les Almées*), the painting shows a harem of belly dancers dancing for their sultan.

of its original elements. An abundance of evidence is found in artwork and written descriptions of the dance that have survived, much of it from ancient sources. What is unique about the belly dance is that its movements are focused in the abdomen, with the legs and arms being used in a subtle way, primarily to enhance the swaying, rotating, shaking, and undulating movements of the torso and hips.

ANCIENT ROOTS

Since religion was once an important part of daily activity, human beings related it to every part of their lives. Virtually all dancing is believed to have begun as a part of worship. The pervasiveness of goddess worship in the ancient Near East is well known. Astarte, Isis, and Aphrodite are just a few prominent figures, and they and many other female deities were often represented in the figures of mothers. It is not surprising that dances performed in worship of these earthy goddesses would have had a strong sexual and reproductive content. It should also be remembered that the role played by men in the creation of life was not fully understood at that time, so the mysterious ability of women to give birth was thought to be a kind of magic. Because of this, women were treated with some degree of fear and respect.

With the advent of Judaism, and later Christianity, goddess worship was suppressed. Women lost much of the status and power they had formerly enjoyed as newly patriarchal (male-dominated) societies began to dictate what activities were appropriate for females in society. Although it was not absolutely forbidden, dance was not closely connected to worship in the new religions and began to evolve into a social pastime to be performed in the home by women who wanted to entertain themselves and each other.

By the time Islam became a powerful religion in the Middle East, the few remaining goddess-oriented faiths were abolished, the temples destroyed, and the freedoms of women restricted more than ever before. However, the people in the mountain and desert villages often quietly adapted the strict rules of Islam to suit their lives because women were needed to help with the flocks and in the fields. It was impossible for their societies to function properly if the women were always closed up in their houses, entirely separate from the men.

The female abdominal dance eventually died out in many parts of the world, but lived on in others, and social dancing among women in the home was tolerated. Public dancing was another matter, and although professionals were hired to entertain for certain types of social events, the spontaneous improvisations of street performers were done by Gypsies and other minorities or the lower classes. The highly polished and educated entertainers who were maintained by royalty and the wealthy in their harems and palaces, however, enjoyed a certain respectability and status.

A unique dance form has evolved from the old. Even in modern times, female abdominal dancing ranges from self-expression for enjoyment in the home—and only among the women—to a popular form of professional public entertainment. The area most closely associated with this type of dancing is still the Arab-Islamic world of its birth.

BELLY DANCING IN MIDDLE EASTERN SOCIETY

Dancing in Middle Eastern society, as in other places in the world, is a means for expressing human emotion. Though we now associate particular costumes with belly dancing, people originally danced in their everyday clothes. What they tied around their hips to emphasize and enhance movement were probably functional items made of substantial material, such as shawls or head coverings. The original purpose of the veil was to modestly cover the woman and was certainly never intended to be removed in a suggestive manner. Scarves and shawls are still frequently tied around the hips in the home or in social gatherings when people dance.

There are many occasions for women to get together to relax and socialize, and it is there that children learn to imitate the dancing without conscious effort. Those who are clever are often singled out to perform for the adults. There is no clear division between audience and performer because they take turns dancing. There is admiration for those who show greater skill or grace, and though there is some technique, each woman has her own style that shows her personality as well as how she carries herself. Everyone is encouraged to participate.

It is somewhat unusual for everyone to dance at once, and more commonly, participants dance as soloists or in pairs. Singing with the music, drumming (either on a percussion instrument or any object at hand), clapping, smiling, and uttering encouraging words and sounds to excite the dancers are a natural part of it all.

This activity is by no means only for the young, for in dancing a woman can celebrate her entire life experience—her maturity adding beauty to the performance. In fact, many of the most revered professional dancers in the Middle East today are well past youth and continue working until the age of 40 or 50, some well into their sixties.

WESTERN PERCEPTIONS OF BELLY DANCING

Following the 1893 World's Fair, the American public was well aware of belly dancing, but still knew nothing of its history or social context in the countries where it had long been part of the culture. Audiences disapproved of, and were at the same time fascinated by, the exotic entertainers from the East. Although there were also many male performers, it was the women who captured the imaginations of Americans. As photographers began to document their performances, so different from Western dances of the day, a postcard trade of "forbidden" women posing in suggestive costumes eventually developed. That perpetuated the Orientalist myth of belly dancers as seductive ladies of the harem dancing for the sultan, an idea that was later further developed by Hollywood.

Just after World War I, the composer Irving Berlin took up the theme in his "Harem Nights," incorporating that same old snake-charmer tune Sol Bloom claimed to have composed when he presented his dancing girls to the press. The tomb of Tutankhamen (King Tut) was discovered around that time, and it created quite a sensation. The spangled net dresses of Egypt created a fashion fad—they were the perfect garments for flappers to wear to perform "the shimmy," which was the most popular dance of the day.

One of the earliest characters to be closely associated with belly dancing in this country was the consummate femme fatale, Salome, a Biblical character. The role of Salome has been danced on the professional stage with amazing frequency. She has also fascinated writers and artists since the Middle Ages, but especially for the past 100 years or so. It was at the height of Salome's popularity in the Roaring Twenties that

Dutch exotic dancer Mata Hari, or Margareta Gertruida Zelle, was probably the most famous woman to dance the role of Salome. Pictured here in Paris in 1905, she was later accused of being a German spy and was executed.

she and her dance became the ultimate symbol of sin and sex. If Salome performed a dance, it would undeniably have been Middle Eastern, but its content will be forever shrouded in mystery with no scholarly evidence to indicate whether it was of the abdominal genre or not.

Some of the most notable women to interpret the role of Salome and the mythical "dance of the seven veils" include Maud Allan, Gertrude

Hoffman, Ruth St. Denis, and Theda Bara. Perhaps the most infamous of all the women to dance the role was Mata Hari. An exotic dancer who was accused of being a German spy, she was finally executed by the French during World War I. Other twentieth-century stereotypes sprang from the many theatrical productions of two other shows with Middle Eastern themes: *Kismet* and the ballet *Scheherazade*.

THE DEVELOPMENT OF CABARET DANCING

The style of dancing often referred to in this country as *cabaret* was developed in the 1920s in Middle Eastern nightclubs, where the performances probably began in response to foreign audiences' demands for this type of entertainment. Egypt had also established itself as the center of the entertainment and film industry in the region, and dancing was incorporated into the story line of nearly all early Egyptian movies. In a bizarre and surprising turn of events, the dancers who were featured in these films adopted a fantasy-style of dance costuming, most often composed of a heavily beaded and sequined bra and belt (*bedleh*), with matching jewelry worn over sheer or semisheer skirts showing a lot of leg. Although this type of costume is particularly associated with Egypt, special theatrical costumes did not originate in the Arab world but were a product of Hollywood. Middle Eastern countries have long restricted dancers from showing their navels. Jewels in the navel, strips of fabric running from the center of the bra to the skirt, and body stockings have all developed in response to that rule.

It was in this same period that the dance began to incorporate more movement in the upper torso and use the arms in new ways, rather than focusing solely on the hips as was customary in more traditional Egyptian dance. As the veil was a garment of modesty in the region, for a dancer to remove the covering publicly would have had serious implications, all of them negative, in that culture. Even when veils were used as part of the act in Egypt, they were only a prop, generally briefly manipulated in a pretty way and then discarded after being carried in the dancers' hands but never worn to cover the body.

In the 1950s, the Broadway production of *Fanny*, starring Turkish dancer Nejla Ates and Egyptian pop singer/musician Mohammed El Bakkar, played to continually packed houses and created the first mass market for Arabic music and dance in the United States. Since then, Middle Eastern music and dance have been found in nightclubs and restaurants of major cities not only in the United States, but also worldwide.

Generally considered to have been the first to introduce Egyptian belly dance to Egyptian films and movies was the late, great Tahia Carioca. She was best known for dancing in the more traditional beledi, or folk style, with movements that were heavy and earthy. In her later years, Carioca gained quite a lot of weight, but her public stayed loyal and loved every inch of her. She danced well into old age, and was much sought after for as long as she performed. Even today she is remembered with admiration and respect, her name synonymous with belly dancing in many Middle Eastern countries.

Samia Gamal was another young and beautiful dancer who achieved fame through her film association (and offscreen romance) with legendary Egyptian singer and actor Farid al-Atrache. Up to that time, dancers had traditionally either gone barefoot or worn flat slippers to protect their feet, but Gamal's innovation of dancing in high-heeled shoes gave her an elegant appearance. Although the real reason she wore the shoes was merely to show that she could afford them, her shoes gave a new and different look to the dance by changing the center of gravity. She eventually married a wealthy Texan and came to the United States. Gamal starred in *Valley of the Kings* in the 1950s—the first American film to feature authentic Egyptian music and dance.

Carioca and Gamal, along with Badia Masabni and Nagua Fouad, were the most prominent dancers of their day and were especially high-profile because they were featured in Egyptian films. Another of the brightest and best-loved stars who danced in Egyptian films was the beautiful Faten Hamama, who was at one time married to actor Omar Sharif. Other dancers who achieved a high level of fame were Nagua Fouad, Farida Fahmi, Hayatem, Aza Sharif, Hind Rostum, Fifi Abdo, and Nelly, as well as Lucy and Dina.

One of the most honored and respected of all the belly dancers has been Suhair Zaki. Known for her fine technical skill and subtlety, and

Egyptian dancer Samia Gamal, pictured here in 1952, first studied under Tahia Carioca but quickly gained a reputation for being a talented solo performer. She would go on to star in dozens of Egyptian films and was later named the National Dancer of Egypt by King Farouk.

for the precision of her hip work, Zaki was also admired for her ability to perform a great variety of movement in a very small space. Her innocent and sweet facial expressions made her appear rather reserved compared with other dancers of her era. Yet her ability to connect with and interpret her music had a huge emotional impact, which awed her audiences and left them breathless with admiration. In a time when most other popular performers relied heavily upon elaborate, even risqué costuming and staging, she never used choreographers or incorporated props of any kind into her shows, but remained the ultimate natural dancer. Indeed, she was often called "Bint el Baled" or "daughter of the country." She retired in the early 1990s while still at the height of her career, but officially came out of retirement in 2001 to teach at the Ahlan Wa Sahlan Festival in Cairo. She has appeared at the festival several times since.

Though many cultures have influenced the oriental dance as it is performed today—and even claim it as their own—its essential characteristics have probably been best retained in Egypt, which is still considered by most people to be the home of belly dancing.

TURKISH BELLY DANCING

There are not only differences in the styles of individual belly dancers, but particular characteristics that vary from country to country. Many countries other than Egypt pride themselves on their own traditions of belly dancing. Generally speaking, though, the other broad style of belly dancing recognized in most Western countries is Turkish. Exhibiting a faster and wilder style, most Turkish dancers are very agile and athletic. They frequently close their performance to music with an irregular beat called *karsilama*, one of several musical influences that likely originated with the Gypsies.

When the Turkish Republic was formed in 1923, the new leader, Kemal Ataturk, created a more secular society to distance the country from the infamy of the Ottomans. Dancing in public was just one of the bold new freedoms that women could enjoy, though there is evidence that Turkish belly dancing had already been in existence for at least 500 years.

One innovation was that rather than remaining in the performance space, dancers would move right out into the audience. Some believe that the highly developed rippling muscular movements of the abdomen—sometimes called belly rolls—originated with Turkish dancers who have never been required to cover their navels. (Many others, however, attribute this type of movement to the Ouled Naïl.) Indeed, they have achieved certain notoriety for their beautiful costumes, often extremely revealing compared to those worn by dancers of other nationalities. Although dancers from many Middle Eastern countries use finger cymbals—called *sagat* in Arabic, and *zilz* in Turkish—Turkish performers are famous for playing them with great skill and dexterity and would not be considered to be good dancers without that ability.

Emine Adalet Pee and Nergis Mogol were among the first famous belly dancers in the newly formed Republic of Turkey, and they were followed by many others in the 1950s, including Nimet Alp, Milike Cermai, and Saliha Tekneci. At the end of the 1950s, Ayse Nana shocked Istanbul by adding striptease to her dance. Sema Yildiz and Inci Birol were famous throughout the Middle East, and many other dancers starred in movies and had songs written in their honor. Ozel Turkbas immigrated to the United States, and during the belly dance fad of the 1970s she produced a series of successful how-to books and music. Turkish dancer Ates Altiok was the featured dancer at "The Astor" in Washington, D.C., for many years, where she fascinated American audiences and students alike with her magnetic personality, physical strength, beauty, and stunningly high-energy performances that typically lasted for a full hour, rather than the more typical 20-minute shows danced by others.

In the following decade, Nesrin Topkapi and Princess Banu were two of the most popular dancers. Burcin Orhon, the daughter of one of Turkey's most famous and beloved composers, is one of the biggest stars of contemporary belly dance. A few other currently popular Turkish belly dancers are Didem, Asena, Tanyeli, and Elcin. In recent years, many upscale restaurants and nightclubs in Turkey have begun to feature beautifully costumed Oriental dance performances of a very high standard. It is interesting, however, that many of them dance to Arabic rather than Turkish music, using props such as canes and candelabras that were once only seen in Egypt. Many of the floor shows also feature several types of traditional Turkish folk dances and also include multilingual singers who delight visitors and provide a wonderfully varied show for their patrons.

Turkish belly dancers are noted for their athleticism, along with a faster and wilder style. Here, a dancer shows her flexibility while performing in Istanbul.

MIDDLE EASTERN DANCE IN THE UNITED STATES

After Middle Eastern dance made its 1893 debut in the United States, the first American dancers were a few daring women who imitated the native performances they had seen at the World's Fair for vaudeville, carnivals, stage shows, and the like. Belly dancers found their way into our very earliest films, beginning with the *Dance of Fatima*, which was shot by Thomas Edison himself. Unfortunately, though, the majority of those first American dancers, many of whom had ballet and jazz training, fell prey to the Orientalist visions of exotic harem beauties. They presented personal interpretations of belly dancing, most of which were far from authentic. However, it was not only American men but also

American women who were intrigued by this mysterious dance of the East that was so unlike Western dancing.

It was not until the late 1960s, though, that the United States experienced a sort of cultural revolution, which included an upsurge in interest in the arts of other cultures. Ethnic restaurants and clubs in large cities finally began to showcase the genuine article: belly dancers from the Middle East who had learned traditionally by watching female friends and family members. Both as performers and teachers, they inspired a generation of American women to don hip scarves and finger cymbals, which eventually led to something new: the American belly dancer.

Representing a cross-section of all social, racial, and economic groups, belly dancers could suddenly be found performing at every conceivable venue. Classes were available in most cities and even offered as courses in colleges and universities. Though in many cases they had little else in common, the women who joined the classes shared a love of expressing their unique femininity through dance. Many American belly dancers are completely unaware of the ancient roots of their dance, and yet many have sensed that what they were experiencing was natural, mysterious, and profound.

One of the most appealing things about belly dancing was and is its accessibility. This was a dance for all women, even those who had always, albeit secretly, wanted to dance but not had the body type or physical ability demanded by traditional Western forms of dance such as ballet. Not a dance only for the slim, belly dancing also suits heavier body types, often allowing the emphasis to be placed on the movements of the hips. Many women are delighted to discover that fuller figures are frequently considered more feminine and attractive in Middle Eastern cultures than the very thin body types so often preferred in modern Western cultures.

Donning a costume for class or performance—even on the smallest of scales—gives the participant something that has become increasingly limited over recent years because of Western society's ever more casual mode of dress: the opportunity to dress up. Wearing exotic clothing made of rich fabrics while embellished with jewelry and makeup makes many women feel more feminine and attractive. This dance tradition with its natural acceptance of all kinds of bodies redefines the meaning of female beauty.

Most American women who dance professionally are underpaid, overworked, and rarely achieve the kind of respect afforded other kinds of dance professionals. Few of them are able to support themselves by dancing alone; they often have other full-time jobs in completely unrelated fields. Many of America's most successful Middle Eastern dancers are not only extremely intelligent, but also highly educated women who would never consider giving up their dancing because of their love for the art. They continue to inspire, as they were once inspired, both in performing and teaching as they pass the torch of their art on to a new generation of dancers.

As religious fundamentalism continues to grow in the lands that gave birth to this unique form of female dance, however, public performance in those countries continues to become increasingly controversial as certain segments of society adhere to very conservative interpretations of Islam. Those beliefs demand that women should be veiled and covered from the view of all men except those who are either their husbands or other immediate family members (brothers, fathers, and sons). There have been unfortunate reports of violence against dancers who have refused to conform to these very strict standards. It is known that many of the most famous Egyptian dancers were at one point forced to surround themselves with entourages of bodyguards to ensure their personal safety, and others have retired because the difficulties have become too great. The number of less famous dancers who used to be paid for performing at weddings and less prestigious nightclubs has declined, and they are frequently replaced by non-Muslim dancers from countries such as Russia, Argentina, the United States, and other Western countries.

Fortunately, while the dance environment in the Middle East has been repressed, it has continued to develop and improve in quality in other places. At this time, there are probably more performers, teachers, and students of belly dancing in the United States than anywhere else in the world, and American dancers have reached the world via seminars, workshops, instructional and performance videos, and books. A huge global dance community has formed and is thriving and constantly growing on the Internet. New dancers everywhere value and are working hard to preserve not only belly dancing, but also a wide range of traditional ethnic dance forms. At the same time, dances continue to

(continues on page 85)

MOROCCO OF NEW YORK

Morocco is the stage name that was given long ago to Carolina Varga Dinicu. In her many years on the dance scene, she has become a highly respected performer and authority in the field of Middle Eastern and North African dance, not only in the United States but also internationally, especially in the Near and Middle East and North Africa.

A member of MENSA (a national organization of individuals with very high IQs), Morocco began college by age 14. Needing a break from the intensity of her intellectual pursuits, she took a class in flamenco, and her eventual excellence at that dance form led her to tour with the Ballet Espanol Ximenez-Vargas. Shortly after returning from her 10-week tour with Espanol Ximenez-Vargas, she was hired to dance at a new Arabic club in New York's Greektown section. She learned Middle Eastern dances on the fly and perfected her art through many hours of practice and immersing herself in Arabic culture.

Although she ultimately decided to devote herself to a career in the dance world, Morocco holds a BA in Modern Languages and an MA in Political Science. She feels that her courses in political science helped immensely in her understanding of the social/political climate of the various countries in which she conducts her dance research. This understanding has also helped her become more familiar with folk forms in an all-encompassing cultural context, and her acute awareness of the many factors that impact a country's dances has led to her concentrate on the authenticity of the dance forms.

She is credited with opening many new doors for Middle Eastern dancers and for being a leading force in elevating their status. Thanks largely to her endeavors, Middle Eastern dance is recognized as a valid, valuable concert

Morocco (real name: Carolina Varga Dinicu) has been one of the main proponents of preserving Middle Eastern dance. Also an accomplished performer, Morocco has won numerous lifetime achievement awards.

form worthy of being presented in churches, libraries, museums, and schools, as well as in other prestigious settings, including the Lincoln Center, the United Nations General

(continues)

(continued)

Assembly, the Dag Hammarskjold Theater, the Delacorte Dance Festival, Columbia University, the Statue of Liberty, the Cooper-Hewitt Museum, and the New York City Department of Cultural Affairs, all of which are venues where she and her troupe have performed. In addition to her many lecture/performances, Morocco has written for a number of publications in her field, and her work has been reprinted in dance, medical, and feminist publications, even internationally.

Morocco has also enjoyed a hugely successful career as an instructor and has taught at SUNY Purchase and Amas Repertory Theater, at workshops throughout the world, and at her own academy in New York City. She has been equally successful as a performer, but she has considered that aspect of her career secondary to her most important life's work: the preservation and presentation of dances that are quickly disappearing from the global artistic landscape. Her research has largely been based upon firsthand observation and interviews of indigenous peoples during a period of more than 50 years. This has given Morocco the opportunity to carefully record what has been changed, lost, or modernized and has given her a basis for comparison and commentary on trends, developments, and influences.

Before the 1964 World's Fair, Morocco made the acquaintance of the former minister of culture of Morocco (one of the two men in charge of the Moroccan Pavilion, where she later danced), an important liaison that also led to an acquaintance with like-minded individuals in Egypt. Through these connections and friendships, she was permitted to visit areas not open to tourists of any kind, where much of life, until recently, had remained unchanged for centuries. Her travels have taken her to many other countries as well, including Tunisia, Algeria, Lebanon, Syria, Jordan, Iraq, Iran, Turkey, Azerbaijan,

Uzbekistan, Turkmenistan, Kazakhstan, Tajikistan, Kirghizia, Georgia, Armenia, Greece, and the country formerly known as Yugoslavia. Morocco has also led many highly successful dance/culture tours to these regions.

There are many skilled and learned dancers in the United States, but what sets Morocco apart is her ability to differentiate between what is real and what is not. She feels there is room for all sorts of creativity and artistry in dance performance, but that dancers—and their audiences—should know what it is they are seeing. In addition, she believes that fantasy and romanticized dances should be identified as what they are and not be presented as authentic ethnic dance.

Showing positive aspects of Middle Eastern cultures is more important than ever, according to Morocco, because this can build bridges between peoples. However, misfortune and economic necessity have led to the breakup of the communal infrastructures that have preserved some dance traditions. It is well known that there are those who now seek to suppress or even eliminate dance—and even those who create them—but Morocco feels that dance and all other forms of art are of immeasurable value and must be saved from extinction.

To that end, she has been able to capture a number of exceptional and breathtaking dances on film, which is invaluable, because all of the performers in the footage are either dead or too old to perform anymore. Because of her work, there exists the only true record of these virtually forgotten ethnic folk dances. Her research video series was presented with the Giza Award in 2000, and an interview with her was commissioned by the Dance Division of the Lincoln Center Library of the Performing Arts in New York to be placed in its Oral History Archives for future

(continues)

(continued)

researchers. She was nominated for the Dance Heritage Coalition's list of "America's Irreplaceable Dance Treasures" as well.

Morocco has acquired a stunning array of accolades from her peers. She was one of the first dancers to be inducted into the American Academy of Middle Eastern Dance (AAMED*)* Hall of Fame, with the designation "World Class" for "International proliferation of her art, her myriad of talent, and for her untiring pioneering in this, her chosen field of ethnic dance." She was named 1997 Instructor of the Year by the International Academy of Middle Eastern Dance (IAMED) and was also honored as Best Dancer and Best Instructor two years running by *Mideastern Dancer* magazine. In addition, her troupe, the Casbah Dance Experience, was also twice named Best Troupe of the Year by the same publication. Morocco was also voted Ethnic Dancer of the Year in 1997 and Instructor of the Year in 1998, and given the Lifetime Achievement award in 2002 by *Zaghareet Magazine*. In 2005, the Middle Eastern Culture and Dance Association (MECDA) awarded her its Humanitarian Award for her "body of work over a lifetime in furthering and enriching Near and Mid-Eastern music and dance." In 2006, the Isis Foundation gave her a Lifetime Achievement Award in Ethnic Dance from the Near and Middle East. In 2009, Morocco was appointed grand marshal of New York's Dance Parade.

While many serious Middle Eastern dancers still shudder about the way Sol Bloom initially marketed his "hootchy-kootchy girls," Morocco points out that we must not forget that in spite of how it was presented, there are likely millions of people who have been made aware of a music and dance tradition from another area of the world due in part to Bloom.

(continued from page 79)

evolve as many experiment with using the ancient movements in new ways. It is to be hoped that dancers from around the world will continue to give new life and meaning to this precious gift from the past.

The most familiar costumes are still modeled on earlier Hollywood styles, which generally involve a bra-type top that is heavily decorated with glittering sequins and beads. The midriff is generally left bare, and a skirt is worn at the bikini line and held in place by a matching belt, with a beaded fringe to accentuate the movements of the dancer. The costume frequently incorporates a large veil, and the dancer often enters with it draped around her in such a way that her body is fully covered, but then later removes it as part of the dance. This is commonly called a cabaret costume.

Variations on these costumes are sometimes made with heavier, more ethnic fabrics and decorated with coins and tassels. Dancers who opt for this look often prefer more primitive music, using acoustic instruments instead of electronic, and might dance flat-footed rather than on the balls of the feet. A dancer who is attempting this look might also incorporate henna decoration on her hands and feet, apply a temporary facial tattoo (*wishem*), and perhaps cover her hair with a scarf or veil to complete the tribal look.

With enduring charm, today's dancer mesmerizes her audience with a unique display of femininity and grace, as did her sisters of yesteryear. A good performer moves in a manner that appears to be effortless, yet creating that illusion requires good technique, great muscle control, and tremendous stamina. It is as demanding as most other forms of dance.

The typical performance in American nightclubs today is divided into distinct sections, each lasting roughly three minutes. The dancer normally enters to lively music, and her costume is often partially or even fully covered by a veil draped around her body in an attractive way. Many dancers also wear and play finger cymbals from the beginning of the performance, which provides interest at a point during which much of the beauty of the costume is still hidden.

The second section is usually performed to slower music. The veil is gracefully removed and manipulated in a dreamy way, as the dancer whirls it around in an amazing variety of movements, often while spinning, before it is finally discarded. Some dancers use this time to engage in playful teasing with a member of the audience; for example, choosing a "victim" and wrapping the veil around his head into a turban, then dancing in front of him. Other dancers carry their veils on, perhaps flowing behind them, manipulate them very briefly, just toss them aside, or simply unceremoniously drop them.

At the end of that section, the music speeds up again and is then followed by the slowest pace in the entire performance. Some dancers improvise undulations on their feet at this point, and others drop to the floor where they might do belly rolls and flutters (called "floor work"). Dancers who use canes, swords, trays of lighted candles, or other props for balancing as part of their acts usually incorporate those items at this point in the dance.

The music again speeds up, and dancers who choose to move out into the audience to seek tips do so at this time. That section is followed by one of the most interesting features: the drum solo. Live music usually makes for the most exciting show, because the drummer comes right out onto the floor and either stands or sits near the dancer. What follows is an exciting improvised duet in which they work as a team. The dancer and the rhythm become one as she follows the beats with her body, the most energy being concentrated in her hips. It is difficult to duplicate this energy with taped music, but a very skilled dancer can come close. The performance culminates in a short, fast finale during which the dancer acknowledges her audience and the musicians, and exits the performance area.

This differs somewhat from the performance of dancers in Egypt. Because it would look as if they are removing their clothing, Egyptian dancers do not wear any kind of veils wrapped around their bodies, but always carry a length of flowing fabric behind themselves for drama during their entrance. It is usually quickly discarded. (Because the veil is a garment of modesty worn by Muslim women around the world, this is a sensitive issue in Egypt.) Egyptian dancers have long been legally prohibited from showing their bare abdomens, and they wear body stockings, usually made of fine mesh or net, or some type of flesh-colored material to match their costumes.

Their dances do not usually have transitions from one section to the next, though the pace and mood of the music sometimes builds in intensity. Many of the most successful dancers have their own orchestras that compose an entire piece of music just for their performance. Within that piece, there is usually some variation in tempo, allowing a variety of movements, but the dancer stays on her feet at all times. Almost all Egyptian dancers finally exit to change to a theatrical version of an appropriate ethnic dress and return to the stage to incorporate some sort of folk dance into their performance. This might include a cane dance (*raqs assaya*), an earthy country dance (*raqs Saidi*), or an impressive show in which the dancer amazes the audience by dancing with a heavy candelabra, candles fully ablaze, balanced on her head (*raqs shamadan*). In another popular finale, the dancer dons a glittering, beautifully embroidered caftan and performs the famous woman's hair dance of the Gulf States (*raqs nasha'at*, also known as *raqs Khaliji*).

Many American dancers are very talented and highly dedicated and trained. Because of their love and appreciation of this beautiful dance, they have gone to great lengths to learn about and understand the culture from which their art form has sprung. There are professional American dancers who speak Arabic, play traditional instruments, and hold degrees in related fields of Middle Eastern studies. A large number have visited the Middle East through tours that are organized especially for dancers.

Still, it could be argued that although dancers from Middle Eastern countries sometimes lack the polish, finesse, and technique of their American imitators, they often have an inborn ease and acceptance of their own bodies, which most Western women lack. Having the added advantage of an innate affinity with and understanding of their own music, their performances often have an added dimension of authenticity and feeling. Those who understand the dance and have seen native dancers perform in Turkey, Lebanon, Algeria, Morocco, and other countries in the Middle East might also make that observation.

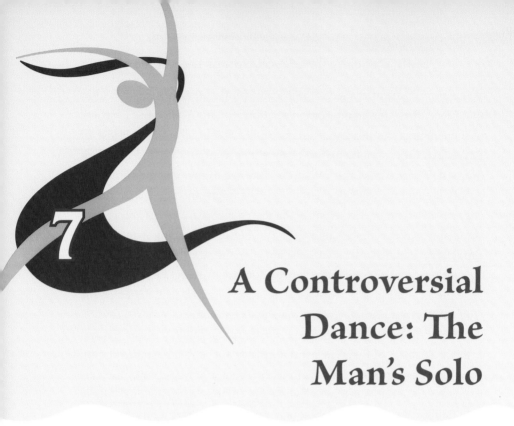

A Controversial Dance: The Man's Solo

The subject of men performing dance solos in public is surprisingly sensitive and has occasionally been the target of harsh and angry criticism by men from Middle Eastern countries, in particular. Perhaps one reason for this is that no people want their cultures and traditions to be misrepresented, especially when they are being presented as authentic. There is likely concern that the undesirable perception of female soloists over their long history might well cause male soloists to be perceived in the same light.

Middle Eastern men are generally very masculine, strong, and proud, and perhaps that is why they are so offended when Westerners (masquerading as Middle Eastern men) present themselves in a way that might be interpreted as effeminate. Yet, there is a considerable body of evidence that there have been many periods in history when men in the Middle East did dance professionally, even as soloists.

MEN'S CABARET

In Western countries, male cabaret dancing is very similar to the female style, borrowing costuming elements such as glitzy fabrics and beaded or coin belts. The first modern male belly dancers were seen in the United States in the late 1960s and 1970s, but their numbers have increased significantly since that time, throughout the world. Male dancers often incorporate some sort of vest with harem pants, a turban, and perhaps a cape. They often use finger cymbals and incorporate balancing swords, canes, or trays of lit candles on their heads, while dancing in a way that is very similar to that of the women. Most Western audiences thoroughly enjoy this sort of show, and most likely never even give a thought to its authenticity or historical precedents.

There are numerous men in the United States today, some of them originally from Middle Eastern countries and others not, who dance beautifully and have been very successful as teachers and performers. This is a trend that is likely to continue.

In many Middle Eastern countries, belly dancing is regarded as a female endeavor and is often frowned upon when males participate in the dance. Pictured here performing in Beirut, Lebanon, is Mousbah Baalbaki, who is one of the few professional male belly dancers in the Middle East.

In nightclubs and at parties, weddings, and other social situations when the type of music that usually initiates belly dancing is played, it is not at all unusual for Middle Eastern men to dance. Both in their home countries and when they are visiting or living in Western countries, they often join the featured dancer, or they dance with their own friends, not only using most of the same movements that women do, but even tying something around their hips for emphasis. Furthermore, if several people are dancing in this manner and one of them happens to be exceptionally good, the others often back off to watch, whether the "expert" is male or female. This type of impromptu performance generally gets a great round of applause from the audience.

However, there is a great difference between dancing in their own street clothes, whether T-shirts and jeans or galabiyas, and donning a costume and appearing as the featured performer. The difference may also lie in whether it is perceived that the dancing is a bit of a spoof on how women dance or whether the dancer is really presenting himself as a woman.

Indeed, the late Ibrahim Farrah danced solo in all sorts of situations and generally was exceedingly well received and highly esteemed by many kinds of audiences, male and female, Western and Eastern. He was a highly respected leader and teacher who did much to promote the art form on many levels. He performed well past his youth. It is an apparent mystery that many of those who would normally object to men dancing in this way accepted and appreciated his performances. It may or may not have been a factor that Farrah actually was of Middle Eastern descent, and that he was a mature and sophisticated person.

It seems that there is a very fine line between what constitutes an acceptable and unacceptable performance, a line that is often invisible to Western dancers and their audiences. One point of importance seems to be that the male dancer should in no way appear feminine. Perhaps where or in what situation the dance is performed as well as how the dancer is costumed and how he deports himself has some bearing on how his dancing is perceived. This may also be related to the old prejudices about dancers in general; although men may accept a woman dancing in a seductive manner, on some deep level, they are embarrassed and unhappy if it is perceived that a man is dancing to entice other men, especially if it has been presented as representative of Middle Eastern culture.

However, many photographs, postcards, and paintings of male dancers have survived, and some of those offer compelling evidence that young boys, dressed rather convincingly as women, did indeed dance professionally in many Middle Eastern countries in the past. It should also be remembered and taken into account that in most of these countries, at one time or another, women were forbidden to dance in public.

In the coffeehouses of eighteenth-century Istanbul, the Kocheks were popular performers. They kept their hair short and wore caps that were known to be masculine, but their clothing strongly resembled what was worn by females of the time. However, they were so popular with the Turkish military personnel (the Janissaries) that they sometimes fought over the Kocheks until the Sultan finally tired of the continual chaos and banished them.

Certainly, there is no doubt that Egypt also had some male dancers (*khawals*) who impersonated women, as evidenced by the writings of Western travelers who visited the country early in the nineteenth century. They filled the void that was left when Muhammed Ali banned the Ghawazee dancers from Cairo. (Some believe that they may even have been the same Kocheks who had been banished from Turkey.) They danced in the manner of the Ghawazee, played finger cymbals, and were hired to entertain for the same sort of events. Although their costumes were somewhat feminine, most of their public realized that they were male and not female. Many of them allowed their hair to grow long and wore it braided, kept their faces free of hair, and even applied kohl to their eyes and henna to their hands like women.

Since Middle Eastern dance made its North American debut at the Chicago World's Fair, male dancers have performed in this country. Perhaps because their female counterparts caused so much public excitement, they were overlooked, but there is no question as to their presence; irrefutable evidence survives in a souvenir book published by the fair, newspaper accounts of the day, and surviving photographs.

There is an additional body of evidence in older movies and videos from the Middle East that contain footage of men who seem to be belly dancing, though they admittedly look entirely masculine and usually dance in their street clothes. Some of the foremost contemporary authorities on Middle Eastern dance have visited the West and have seemed surprised but not offended by seeing other men perform cabaret-type solos. Male dancers are not only tolerated, but well liked in modern Turkey, where Evrim Sultan is an award-winning dancer; he is just one of several popular performers who have been featured on television.

Many of those who have opportunities to spend time in Middle Eastern countries or even in the company of people from that part of the world have had the experience of witnessing the spontaneous, natural dancing done by almost everyone: men and women, young and old alike. Most, if not all, of the movements that comprise the genre we have labeled belly dancing are as natural as breathing.

New York dancer Tarik Sultan has made significant contributions in documenting the history of the male role in Middle Eastern dance. His article "Oriental Dance, It Isn't Just for Women Anymore" is a great source on the history and culture of Middle Eastern dance. Sultan is also much sought after as a performer.

While belly dancing is firmly entrenched in Egyptian culture, there aren't many acclaimed performers. Perhaps the most famous Egyptian man to perform as a professional belly dancer is Tito Seif, who enjoys great popularity when he performs in Egypt's popular resort town Sharm el Sheikh in the Sinai. He is also much in demand for weddings and special events in other major cities. Seif performs in the traditional loose-fitting galabiya, with a scarf tied around his hips so that his movements can be seen. Although he uses the same dance vocabulary as his female counterparts, his dancing is powerful and clearly masculine. Seif gives a wonderful representation of the very best of authentic dance and demonstrates great technical skill as well as a contagious joy. (A 2005 recording of him performing in Giza can be seen on YouTube at http://www.youtube.com/watch?v=6autbeh_tUk.)

Regardless of their ancient origins, and however often they are misinterpreted, the movements articulated by belly dancers can be a wonderful expression of joy for all people, from every part of the world, and for all of time.

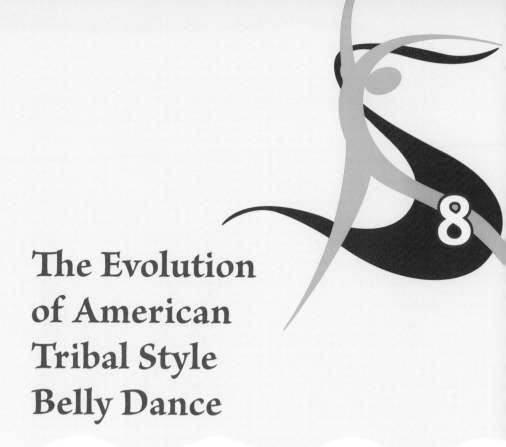

The Evolution of American Tribal Style Belly Dance

During the past 50 years, the San Francisco Bay Area has become the epicenter of a relatively new, uniquely American incarnation of belly dance. It is the birthplace of what has been called California tribal, and/or American tribal style (ATS), belly dance. Unlike the more traditional Egyptian cabaret style, it is a fusion of ethnic styles, clearly Middle Eastern in appearance and feeling, but colored by American innovations in costuming, choices of music, and manners of presentation.

A NEW TYPE OF BELLY DANCE

Jamila Salimpour was the first to bring this new style of belly dance to the public's attention in a significant way, and it is she who is widely acknowledged to have begun the belly dance revival in the United States. While serving in Egypt with the Sicilian military, her father had seen Ghawazee dancers perform. It impressed him deeply, and it was his descriptions of what he saw that first made her aware of the dance form. Salimpour was further exposed to Middle Eastern dancing in movies she watched with her Egyptian landlady, who was another excellent source of firsthand information. Salimpour began performing herself in the 1960s and eventually became the owner of the Bagdad Cabaret on Broadway, where she had the opportunity to observe and question dancers hired from different countries in the Middle East. All these experiences gave her access to a vast amount of information, which she articulated and passed on to students in an organized manner, something no one had ever done before. She is widely credited with being the first to actually name the movements and develop a real vocabulary for this style of dance.

Although Salimpour initially taught the cabaret-style dance typically seen in Middle Eastern nightclubs, by 1968, she had formed an entirely new kind of troupe that was well suited to outdoor performance at the Renaissance Pleasure Faire in northern California. Her newly formed group, Bal-Anat, followed a format Salimpour had learned during her teen years as an acrobat with the Ringling Brothers' Circus. With their performances, Salimpour attempted to create the look of an Arabian variety show as she imagined it might look at a festival or a souk. The entire troupe appeared onstage together, then engaged in a series of short, sequential performances representing old-style dancing from many areas of the Middle East; musicians who played the music were also part of her troupe. Ouled Naïl, tray dances performed by men, Algerian water glass dances, Tunisian pot dances, sword dances, mask dances, snake dances, and even magicians were all part of the show. They were presented alongside the more typical female solo, with all performers wearing costuming appropriate to the region and dance they were representing. The troupe was identified to their audiences as American tribal in an attempt to make it clear that these dancers were Americans and that they were modifying their dancing to suit the expectations of fairgoers. However, they looked as though they were indeed members of a tribal village and were so believable that audiences were often confused and thought what they were seeing was true Middle Eastern dance. What they created was so impressive that their style of performance and dress was soon being widely imitated throughout the United States, even though most of their imitators—like those who saw their performances—did not realize that Bal-Anat's performances were not entirely authentic.

Masha Archer was a former student of Salimpour's who put her own stamp on the new style by not distinguishing between the regions and simply identifying it all as belly dance. She founded the San Francisco Classic Dance Troupe, which existed for 14 years. Archer was unwilling to perform in bars and restaurants and undoubtedly raised awareness that belly dance can be presented as theater and in venues where people go with an expectation of seeing respectable performance art. She felt the dance was timeless—that it was so lovely, special, and worthy of respect that her nonauthentic innovations were forgivable. Archer believed that because of the mixed or even negative attitudes Middle Eastern people had toward the dance and the women who perform it, belly dance deserved to be adopted by the American women who loved and honored it so much. Her background as a painter and a sculptor perhaps contributed to her taking inspiration from the traditional dance, but she was not opposed to altering it in whatever manner felt right to her. Likewise, her costume choices were far more eclectic than those of the earlier tribal dancers, although to most Americans, they appeared to be authentic because of her use of real tribal jewelry and antique pieces. Her attitude toward music was much the same; rather than confining her choices to the usual popular and traditional selections, she experimented with using a variety of types of music.

FATCHANCEBELLYDANCE

Carolena Nericcio, director of FatChanceBellyDance (FCBD), is a dancer who began her journey with Masha Archer, and it was she who ultimately created a truly modern and standardized style of "tribal" dance. She originally began teaching so that she could have dance partners after Archer's San Francisco Classic Dance Troupe disbanded. To some extent, Nericcio and her dancers were isolated from the influences of others for a time, and that was a factor in allowing them to develop a very new look.

FatChanceBellyDance was founded by Carolena Nericcio (*seen here performing in 2008*) in the late 1980s in San Francisco, California.

Nericcio created cues for particular steps or combinations of steps. The cues were subtle changes in arm or head positions that could easily be seen by those who were following her or another dancer designated as leader. All steps began with gestures to the right, so dancers angled slightly left in order to see and follow the lead dancer. The end result was a performance that appeared to be carefully choreographed and rehearsed, but it was in fact improvised. Nericcio has also taught her students to respect the wisdom and generosity of their teachers and to respect and take pleasure from dancing with one another. The ATS dancers are known for their posture and dignified and graceful style of movement.

Although Nericcio and her troupe favored the heavy costuming used by Jamila Salimpour, there was uniformity among the dancers more akin to Archer's style. Their costuming is constantly evolving, but ATS dancers are widely associated with heavy turbans, decorated with flowers and antique jewelry; coin bras worn over cholis; and mirrored, fringed, and tasseled belts worn over layers of very full "fluffy" skirts over pantaloons. There is heavy use of authentic ethnic fabrics and antique jewelry, as well as a distinctive style of makeup that includes facial tattooing modeled after real tribal markings.

Another innovation Nericcio brought to the new style was body art. It was perhaps initially coincidence, but primitive body adornment was becoming fashionable on the West Coast, and Nericcio was tattooed. By chance in some cases, choice in others, many of those who joined her were tattooed as well, some of them quite heavily. Because of this, Nericcio and her dancers became a visible presence at tattoo shows and conventions in the Bay Area, to the extent that this also became an important element in the ATS "look." It was something that set the troupe apart from what was traditional among those who performed belly dance in the United States and among indigenous belly dancers.

Nericcio and FCBD have kept their movements within the standard belly dance repertoire. Those steps are detailed on their *Tribal Basics* video, and include the following:

- Basic Egyptian (Step Touch with a hips swivel forward and back)
- Choo-choo (Sliding Hip Lift—slide foot out on demi-pointe, hip up, slide other foot to meet, hips to neutral)
- Taxeem (Vertical figure eight with the hips, accent on the up)
- Reverse Taxeem (Maia: a vertical figure eight with the hips, accent on the down)
- Shimmy (3/4 shimmy, alternating hips up, and a triplet count 1-2-3-rest)
- Arabic (Camel: full-body undulation leading with the chest— like a full-body figure eight)

The group strongly favors North African and Middle Eastern folkloric music. While Nericcio acknowledges the cultural context of the dance, she believes that American Tribal Style is here to stay, and it will continue to evolve to meet the expectations of the audience—as it always has done.

OTHER TRIBAL DANCE GROUPS

There are many highly successful and distinctive teachers and troupes, and each group brings its own touches and innovations to the dance, but there are several particularly noteworthy proponents of tribal style of dance. Hahbi 'Ru is another Bay Area troupe of Middle Eastern dancers and musicians with tribal leanings. Codirectors John Compton and Rita Alderucci were also once students of Jamila Salimpour and also soloists with her troupe Bal-Anat during the early years. Because they have been influenced by the music and dances of many others, they also borrowed their name from the Bedouin tribes who once wandered the deserts taking what they wanted from those they encountered in their travels. They have been performing together and adding their own unique flavor to the folkloric style since 1991.

Located in Hawaii, Black Sheep Belly Dance was founded by Kajira Djoumahna, the author of one of the best sources on ATS, *The Tribal Bible: Exploring the Phenomenon That Is American Tribal Style Bellydance*. Djoumahna is able to perform many traditional dance forms but has devoted her career to the proliferation of ATS belly dance. She was drawn to it because of its unlimited possibilities as a modern take on ancient dance, but even more, for its ability to develop community among dancers, which builds self-esteem among dancers—not through competition but through cooperation as they work together to perform improvisational dancing. Djoumahna studied with Carolena Nericcio of FCBD and spent eight years as a student and member of her various performance troupes. Other teachers who influenced her greatly include Elizabeth Artemis Mourat, Delilah, Suhaila and Jamila Salimpour, TerriAnne, Deanne Adams, Tempest, Rachel Brice, Laurel Victoria Gray, Morocco, and Sarala Dandekar. She and her husband, Chuck, are co-producers of the award-winning Tribal Fest, the first, and likely still the largest, five-day dance event for ATS. Perhaps her most notable achievement has been authoring the informative *Tribal Bible*, a book that has been so successful that all three of its printings have rapidly sold out. It is currently the most complete and comprehensive documentation of the tribal movement in print, filled with interviews with major dancers, history of the dance, and details about textiles, jewelry, music, and movements, all illustrated with more than 300 photographs.

Paulette Rees-Denis, director of the Gypsy Caravan, is widely acknowledged to have brought tribal belly dance to the Pacific Northwest. She has been teaching and performing in Portland, Oregon, since 1991, and in 2000, she opened Caravan Studio—A World of Dance, along with her husband and fellow group member, Jeff Rees. Rees-Denis directs Tribal Quest NorthWest, a five-day festival of tribal-inspired music and dance in Portland, and also publishes a quarterly international journal, *Caravan Trails*, with art, interviews, reviews, and more about tribal and related dance styles. She is also the author of *Tribal Vision: A Celebration of Life through Tribal Belly Dance*. Gypsy Caravan—and its offshoot, Mizna—is not only composed of dancers, but the group also includes musicians of diverse backgrounds who perform original compositions, which are a blend of music from North Africa, Spain, India, and the Middle and Near East, using a variety of instruments. They have several popular CDs on the market and are much in demand for a variety of performances.

Yet another manifestation of the tribal movement in the United States is known as tribal fusion. This category includes dancers who draw from the ATS style but do not necessarily improvise their performances and often perform as soloists as well as in groups. While the inspiration is clearly belly dance, fusion dancers show more individuality in their costuming and choices of music, and often heavily incorporate influences from other forms of dance and fashion. Indian, flamenco, and African dance are often fused with Middle Eastern in this style. Another popular and relatively new trend involves the incorporation of elements of modern, hip-hop, and funk stylings into movement and costuming. Those who are following these fashions are often labeled urban tribal dancers.

One of the most recent variations of this particular genre has been spearheaded by Rachel Brice and her troupe, the Indigo Belly Dance Company. Using world fusion and industrial music, as well as more traditional accompaniments, the dramatically costumed dancers utilize extremely slow, controlled undulations of the torso and arms punctuated

One of the most innovative tribal fusion style belly dancers is Rachel Brice of San Francisco. In 2003, she founded the Indigo Belly Dance Company, which performs throughout the United States.

by pop and lock movements, while their faces remain relatively sober, sometimes even deliberately detached and expressionless. Many dancers of this ilk favor industrial and Gothic fashion expressions. This is an edgy style with many new adherents, and it seems to evolve at a more rapid pace than most other fusion dances. Not surprisingly, it is somewhat controversial among more traditional dancers.

While the tribal belly dance movement is rooted in and driven from the West Coast, dancers throughout the United States have steadily been developing other tribal styles and often achieve the same sort of look, but through choreography rather than improvisation. Just as the tribal movement was born in a West Coast renaissance fair, so has it continued to grow and evolve in similar venues all the way to the East Coast, where it is still very often found at Society of Creative Anachronism events, such as the Pennsic Wars. Because this is the newest incarnation of belly dancing, terminology is constantly developing and can vary greatly from one area to another; though, it seems clear that this new American cousin of the ancient dance is becoming an important genre, not only in the United States, but throughout the world.

Although Suhaila Salimpour does not fit neatly into the tribal category, a significant number of high-profile tribal dancers have done at least some of their training with the second-generation belly dancer. Salimpour is a much sought-after performer and teacher who has used talent, vision, and creativity to build a very successful business. She is a second-generation belly dancer, the daughter of dance pioneer Jamila Salimpour and Ardeshir Salimpour, a Persian drummer. Suhaila began her dance training with her mother at the age of 2 and later also studied other forms of dance, including jazz, tap, and ballet as well as modern forms such as hip-hop. She was already working as an instructor and professional performer by the age of 14.

Like her mother before her, Salimpour feels that for this dance form to continue to grow and thrive, it must have a solid technique, a format, and a common language. Her intention is to give her students such a strong dance foundation that those who study with her will be equipped to take their dancing in many directions. To facilitate this, she has created an organized and progressive system for teaching that integrates Middle Eastern dance with modern forms. She has also founded a highly acclaimed certification program called the Suhaila Salimpour Format.

She has very successfully used technology to make online dance classes available worldwide and has produced many instructional, fitness, and performance videos. In addition, she directs the Suhaila Salimpour School of Dance and the Suhaila Dance Company and has created a new incarnation of her mother's famous tribal dance company, Bal-Anat. Producer Miles Copeland has worked with Salimpour in a series of performances, videos, and films for the Belly Dance Superstars and has featured her and her work in his movie *The American Belly Dancer*.

Salimpour has toured Canada and Europe as well as the Middle East, where she was very warmly received; she was also the first belly dancer featured by Arab American Television. In addition, she was artistic director and producer of the dance show *Sheherezade*, and her performance in that glittering theatrical production netted her a nomination for a prestigious Izzy Award (named for modern dancer Isadora Duncan). Salimpour has appeared on several American television series, including *Fame, Max Headroom*, and an ABC pilot entitled *Harem*. She was the featured dancer at the prestigious Arabic nightclub Byblos, in Los Angeles, for six years. Salimpour's goal is to see Middle Eastern dance achieve the same respect and loyalty that other dance forms have achieved and to continue to prepare her students to be dancers for life.

Two Examples of Middle Eastern Dance Movements

There are endless variations of the dabkeh that are based on the country, or region, of origin, or even family. The steps are sometimes named accordingly—for example, Al-Baalbakieh for the people of Baalbeck in eastern Lebanon, or Al-Shmaliah for the people from the north. The speed of the dance is determined by the speed of the music. One of the most basic and simple six-beat figures would be:

> With knees slightly flexed, bodies close together, hands clasped and arms ramrod straight, and weight on the right foot, always moving to the right;
>
> Left foot crosses in front of right foot;
>
> Right foot steps right, slightly behind the left foot that has just crossed in front of it;
> Left foot crosses in front of right foot;

Right foot steps right, slightly behind the left foot that has just crossed in front of it;

Low kick with left foot while sort of hopping onto right foot to bear weight;

Stamp (or stamps) with left foot (but then quickly take weight off left foot and put it back onto the right foot as sequence will repeat and left foot will again cross in front of right);

Repeat.

This might also be written as

step(l), step(r),
step(l), step(r),
kick(l)/hop(r) at the same time,
stomp(l) quick-step(r)
repeat

BELLY DANCE

Oriental (belly) dance has a general vocabulary of movements that are used by most dancers. Although there are currently several teachers and schools that are making real progress toward standardizing the dance vocabulary and making it more uniform, the names of these movements are not yet entirely regulated and can vary from one place to another, especially depending upon where and from which teacher they have been learned. Every part of the body can be used, though the legs and feet are used to help create the illusion of fluidity and are rarely the focus of attention as is usual in other forms of dance. Dancing on the flat of the foot is usually considered folkloric, while classical danse orientale is normally performed on the balls of the feet. The many movements that are combined to make up this fascinating dance are best learned by watching good performers and taking lessons. Some have been able to learn from watching videos. There are now some excellent courses available online as well, though in studying in this fashion, students lose the opportunity of having the teacher actually observe what they are doing and make corrections.

Most movements can be classified as either isolations or undulations. When one part of the body is moved separately, it is isolated, and the rest of the body is still so that attention is focused on the moving part(s). An undulation generally involves several parts of the body moving in a smooth, wavelike motion. Nearly any part of the body can move in both isolated and undulated figures, though this requires a mastery of muscles that is usually best acquired through a combination of instruction and practice.

Perhaps the most easily recognized family of movements would be those that are concentrated in the area of the hips, where the emphasis is often either on upward or downward thrusts. In many circles, when the hips thrust or pop up, they are often, but not always, referred to as Turkish, and when they focus on downward movement, they are likewise commonly labeled Arabic. Hip movements can also twist and circle and roll, and they can include rapid vibrations called shimmies. Most common movements alternate between hips, but others emphasize one hip exclusively.

Undulations are probably most closely associated with the dance, and they can be performed either side to side or front to back. In one common movement, the dancer actually creates the look of the rolling gait of the camel by gently swaying the entire torso front to back, with the hips lagging slightly behind, while walking, a movement that can also be executed while turning in a slow circle or simply standing in place. Some skilled performers are able to combine this with raising and lowering the rib cage to allow fluid and alternating movement between the diaphragm and the lower abdomen to create the look of a belly roll, though a true belly roll requires alternately contracting and releasing the upper and lower abdominal muscles in a continuous movement that can roll top to bottom, or vice versa. Figure eights can also be traced, either horizontally or vertically, in a smooth and pretty way, often combined with both large and small hip circles.

Nearly all movements can be executed while traveling, or moving around the performance space, or remaining in one spot in a fixed

A variety of interesting and beautiful movements of the hands and arms comprise the dance vocabulary of belly dance. Author Penni AlZayer is pictured here dancing in a typical Saidi costume.

position. Being able to travel around the space can be important, especially because dancers often perform surrounded by their audiences, rather than just to the front as in a theatrical venue. Many dancers also incorporate much turning into their performances, and this can range from slow simple turns to more complicated high-speed whirling, and some circle the floor with a foot pattern that takes them in one direction while their bodies are spinning in the opposite direction. This is particularly effective if the dancer is carrying a cape or veil, as it can be made to whirl in an endless variety of configurations.

Most movements are done standing on the feet, whether still or traveling, but it is also possible to do both types of movements from other positions. Some dancers make the transition from the fast segment of the dance preceding floor work by executing a very fast spin, and then collapsing onto their backs or by making a whirling descent to land in a facedown position. When the slower music begins, they move from the landing position often to the knees, dancing all the while until they finally gradually rise and return to the standing position. Many performers choose to incorporate tricks such as belly rolls and flutters while lying on their backs, and others balance swords or trays of lighted candles on their heads at this point. Floor work is illegal in some Middle Eastern countries, so performers who are striving for authenticity often eliminate it from their repertoire. Floor work can be performed with grace and elegance, but it can also look suggestive if not executed carefully and tastefully.

There are a variety of interesting and beautiful movements of the hands and arms in the dance vocabulary, and also of the shoulders and rib cage. In most cases, the arms are kept soft and held out and away from or above the body. They can either frame or draw attention to the moving area, such as the hips, or become the moving area. The hands sometimes move in an extension of that rippling or framing effect, or they may be occupied with finger cymbals. The shoulders can be used, both for subtle shimmies and shakes, sometimes in rhythm to emphasize a particular feature in the music. The rib cage is sometimes forcefully pushed up or slammed down in movements likely borrowed from folk forms but used very effectively to accent rhythm.

Facial expression can be very important in establishing the mood of the dance, and many performers use cosmetics to draw attention to the eyes and give them the black-rimmed exotic look that has been associated with the Middle East since Pharaonic times. It is common for dancers to slide their faces and/or their eyes side to side, sometimes rhythmically and often with exaggerated fluttering eyelashes, especially when using veils in the performance. A dancer can also draw attention to the most subtle of movements, such as a belly roll or tummy flutter, or even an isolated vibrating hip, by staring at it, even feigning surprise—an effect that is sometimes used for humor.

A very simple hip movement would involve bumping the hip in one direction. Keeping the hands soft, raise the left arm straight up over the head, and extend the right arm straight out to the right side (horizontal to the floor) with the palm facing up. Standing on the balls of the feet, with the weight on the left foot, and knees relaxed, step to the right with the right foot, and bump the right hip to the right, as though you are using your hip to close a drawer. Quickly bring the left foot over to meet the right in its new position, and repeat this movement eight times. This can be accentuated by looking to the right or even down at your right hip, and the right hand can also be rotated at the wrist with each flip. That entire sequence can then be reversed and repeated to the left.

Another simple movement that could be added would be to lead with the right foot and turn to the right for three counts and shake the shoulders on the fourth count, then reverse the sequence and repeat it to the left, leading with the left foot. The arms should be held out and away from the body during the turns. Raising both arms above the head in a relaxed position with soft hands, and with weight on the flat left foot, bend the right knee and put the toe of the left foot right beside it. This will cause the right hip to be in a raised position. Slam the right hip down toward the floor, quickly raise it back up, and repeat another three times. As the strong downward movement is emphasized, what is seen will be four right hip drops. That move should then be reversed and repeated four times on the left hip, then once again on the right and again on the left.

A slightly more difficult sequence would be to put both arms up and hands behind the head, and with weight on the flat left foot, slightly rock forward onto the right tiptoe. When shifting the weight from the left to right foot, lift the rib cage up and out. After that, weight is shifted back onto the left foot, and there is a slight rocking movement back as the rib cage comes down and back to its original position. The knees and back should be kept very relaxed, and with practice, this becomes a rolling, undulating sort of motion. This can be combined with slowly turning to the right with each step onto the right tiptoe until a full circle is made to eight counts.

The aforementioned three sequences can be combined into many combinations of movements that can be slightly altered and rearranged by changing the position of the arms, the emphasis of the hips, or the direction of the body to form a very simple dance.

CHRONOLOGY

B.C.

Dancing is an integral part of predominant goddess worship in the Near East, a trend that lessened with the advent of Judaism, Christianity, and Islam.

1500   Miriam, the sister of Moses, dances to celebrate the destruction of the Egyptians.

A.D.

32   Salome dances before Herod Antipas at her mother's request and is rewarded with the head of John the Baptist.

600   Gypsy tribes likely move from northern India into the Middle East, where they become famous as traveling street entertainers. (In Egypt, they are called Ghawazee.)

1273   Mevlana Jalaluddin Rumi dies, and the brotherhood of Whirling Dervishes is formally founded by his son.

1650   Wealthy travelers to the Middle East make written records describing Egyptian dancers.

1720   Male dancers (Kocheks) entertain in coffeehouses in Istanbul.

1798   Napoleon leads expedition to Egypt, and soldiers and historians encounter the Ghawazee, after which 400 of them are executed and others confined and controlled by the French army.

1800   Male dancers (*khawals*) are seen in Egypt by Western travelers.

1881   A dancer who calls herself Fatima plays the Birdcage Saloon in Tombstone, Arizona.

1888   Rimsky-Korsakov composes his most famous work, an orchestral suite called *Sheherazade*, based upon the legendary collection of Middle Eastern fairy tales called *A Thousand and One Arabian Nights*.

1889   Sol Bloom first sees Middle Eastern dancers at the Paris Exposition Universelle.

1893   The Chicago World's Fair/Columbian Exposition, where the American public first sees authentic Middle Eastern dancers, is held. Attractive French dancers perform at the Persian Palace wearing skimpy costumes and draw huge crowds to see a fantasy version of Oriental dance.

1894   A performer called Madame Ruth is featured in a kinetograph entitled *Dance du Ventre*.

1897   An authentic-looking performance entitled *Fatima's Dance* is filmed at Coney Island, New York.

1903   Maud Allan makes her acting and dancing debut in *Vision of Salome*.

1906   A dancer who calls herself "Little Egypt" is associated with a scandalous performance at the Awful Seeley Dinner that ends in a police investigation and is later parodied by Oscar Hammerstein on Broadway in a burlesque show called *Silly's Dinner*.

1907   Gertrude Hoffman's show is stopped because of her "indecent" dancing in the role of Salome.

1910   Ted Shawn, husband of legendary dancer Ruth St. Denis, first sees the dancers of the Ouled Naïl.

1911   The Middle Eastern play *Kismet* is written by Edward Knoblock.

1915   Theda Bara fabricates a Middle Eastern background and image and eventually stars in silent films such as *Salome* and *Cleopatra*.

1922   The tomb of Tutankhamen (King Tut) is discovered by archaeologists, and a new wave of interest in all things Middle Eastern begins.

1925   Kemal Ataturk abolishes the dervish orders and turns their monasteries into museums as part of his plan to modernize Turkey and distance it from the Ottoman Empire. Due to his reforms, women are now permitted to dance in public.

1931   Chicago philanthropist Charles Crane officially visits the newly formed Kingdom of Saudi Arabia, where the son of the first ruler, King Abdul Aziz, performs the *al Ardhah* in his honor.

1936   Little Egypt is presented as a lewd character in the motion picture *The Great Ziegfeld*.

1948   Congressman Sol Bloom denies that there was ever a dancer called Little Egypt at the Chicago World's Fair.

1953   The play *Kismet* is adapted and opens as a hugely popular Broadway musical featuring Whirling Dervishes and belly dancers.

1954   Samia Gamal stars in *Valley of the Kings*, the first American film to feature authentic Middle Eastern music and dance.

The dervish orders are again permitted to practice openly in order to preserve a historic tradition of Turkey.

Fanny opens at the Majestic Theatre on Broadway and features Turkish belly dancer Necla Ates and Egyptian musician Mohammed El Bakkar.

1958   Ayse Nana shocks Istanbul by adding striptease to her dance.

1960   The cultural revolution begins and awakens a revival of interest in all things ethnic, including Middle Eastern dance and music.

1968   Jamila Salimpour creates Bal-Anat and brings the American version of tribal style costuming and dance to the Renaissance Pleasure Faire in northern California.

1970   Turkish dancer Ozel Turkbas immigrates to the United States and produces how-to books and music in response to the belly dance fad.

1975   Ibrahim Farrah publishes the first issue of the highly respected Middle Eastern dance magazine *Arabesque*.

An international dance community begins to grow and continues to flourish via many excellent publications, ongoing workshops, seminars and organizations for dancers, and most recently, the Internet.

1987   Carolena Nericcio forms FatChanceBellyDance (FCBD) and American tribal style, which blends the costuming and stage formats of her teachers, Masha Archer and Jamila Salimpour. The American tribal revolution begins in earnest.

1996   Suhaila Salimpour continues the work of her mother, Jamila; she forms a school of belly dance and implements the first formal certification program in Middle Eastern dance.

1999   Kajira Djoumahna publishes *The Tribal Bible: Exploring the Phenomenon That Is American Tribal Style Bellydance*. A definitive history of the dance in the United States, the first edition includes more than 300 photographs and quickly sells out.

2002   Miles Copeland forms the Bellydance Superstars, a professional American belly dance troupe that has toured North America, Europe, and Asia, bringing a distinctly American take on belly dance in many incarnations to the mainstream throughout the world.

2003   The Ministry of Manpower and Immigration bans non-Egyptians from obtaining belly dancing licenses. That ban is reversed a year later with the result that many foreign dancers, especially Russians, are now working in Egypt.

The second edition of *The Tribal Bible: Exploring the Phenomenon That Is American Tribal Style Bellydance* quickly sells out and is now out of print. Very expensive copies of the book can occasionally be purchased used.

Indigo Belly Dance Company is founded by Rachel Brice.

2006   Isis Foundation presents Morocco with its Lifetime Achievement Award in Ethnic Dance from the Near and Middle East, one of several lifetime achievement awards earned by Morocco.

2007   Brice's dance troupe, Indigo Belly Dance Company, is featured in its first full-length touring show, *Le Serpent Rouge*, which is presented by producer Miles Copeland.

GLOSSARY

al Ardhah   Men's battle dance of Saudi Arabia

al ras   A very large bass drum

American Tribal Style (ATS)   A style of belly dancing that includes a fusion of ethnic styles (not just Egyptian cabaret style); it is clearly Middle Eastern in origin, but there are American influences in costumes, music choice, and presentation style. It is performed by Carolena Nericcio and FatChanceBellyDance.

awalem   Learned woman (singular *almeh*)

ayyalah   Men's battle dance from the Arabian Gulf countries

bisht   Outer garment worn on formal occasions by men in the Gulf countries

bokhur   Incense or perfume made from aromatic gums

dabkeh   Famous line dance of the Levant

daff or duff   Flat, round hand drum

danse du ventre   Literally "dance of the stomach" in French

darbuka   Goblet-shaped hand drum

dishdasha   Long, flowing caftan-like garment of the United Arab Emirates

djinn   Middle Eastern fairies (singular *djini*, or "genie" in English)

galabiya   Loose, floor-length robe worn in Egypt

Ghawazee   Egyptian dancers of Gypsy origins (singular *Ghaziya*)

ghutra   Cloth used for covering men's heads in the Gulf countries

guedra   A simple kitchen pot, sometimes used as a drum

haram   Forbidden

harem   Area where women and children are secluded

henna   A paste used for cosmetic/medicinal purposes since ancient times

horabah   A verse or short melody to prepare men for battle

iqal   Coils worn to hold male head coverings in place

kanun   A plucked stringed instrument that is the predecessor of the harp and piano

karsilama   A 9/8 Turkish rhythm of Gypsy origin

kemenja   A bowed fretless lute

Khaliji   Adjective meaning from the Arabian Gulf (noun *Khalij*)

khawal   A boy who imitates the women's dance

kohl   Oil of antimony used as eyeliner since ancient times

kudum   A pair of small kettledrums

kufiyah   A small, white crocheted cap (also called *taghiyah*)

Levant   Area comprised of Israel, Jordan, Lebanon, Palestine, and Syria

mizmar   Middle Eastern horn with a whiny sound, similar to an oboe

mutribah   Leader of female band who usually plays oud and sings

nay or ney   Bamboo Arabic flute

Oriental   From the East, often understood as Middle Eastern

Orientalists   Artists and writers whose work represented fantasies of Middle Eastern people and cultures

oud   Arabic stringed instrument without frets and the predecessor of the lute

Persian   Iranian

raqs   Saidi dance of the countryside (southern or Upper Egypt)

raqs al beledi   Arabic for "dance of the people" or "of the country"

raqs al khawanem   Arabic for "dance of the ladies"

raqs assaya   Egyptian stick dance, usually performed by women

raqs nasha'at   Women's dance from the Gulf countries, also called the hair dance

raqs sha'abi   Folk dance

raqs sharqi   Dance of the East or Orient

raqs tanbur   Egyptian secular form of the whirling dance

ras   The person who leads the dabkeh

rebaba   A bowed, single-stringed instrument with a coconut shell body

sagat   Finger cymbals (Arabic)

Saidi   From Upper (southern) Egypt

Saudi   From Saudi Arabia

semâ   The whirling dance of the dervishes

shimmy   A rapid vibrating up-and-down or side-to-side motion

souk   Bazaar or market

tabla   A simple drum

taghiyah   A small, white crocheted cap (also called *kufiyah*)

tahtib   Battle dance of Egyptian men

takhmir   Drum used in ayyalah

tanbur   A lute with frets

taqsim   Musical improvisation, usually either a solo or featuring one instrument

tar   Tambourine

thobe   Garment traditionally worn by men in the Gulf countries

thobe neshal   Decorative garment worn for performance of raqs nasha'at

tubul   Drum

zar   A dance performed in Egypt that involves achieving an ecstatic trancelike state

zhagareet   Ululating sound of joy or approval

Zikr   The ceremony performed by the Whirling Dervishes

zilz   Finger cymbals (Turkish)

BIBLIOGRAPHY

Adams, Doug, and Diane Apoltolos-Cappadona. *Dance as Religious Studies*. New York: The Crossroad Publishing Company, 1993.

Al-Rawi, Rosina-Fawzia. *Grandmother's Secrets—The Ancient and Healing Power of Belly Dancing*. New York: Interlink Books, 1999.

Appelbaum, Stanley. *The Chicago World's Fair of 1893*. New York: Dover Publications Inc., 1980.

Buonaventura, Wendy. *Serpent of the Nile—Women and Dance in the Arab World*. New York: Interlink Books, 1998.

Carlton, Donna. *Looking for Little Egypt*. Bloomington, Ind.: IDD Books, 1994.

Djoumahna, Kajira. *The Tribal Bible: Exploring the Phenomenon That Is American Tribal Style Bellydance*. Santa Rosa, Calif.: Kajira Djoumahna/ BlackSheep BellyDance, 2003

Friedlander, Shems. *The Whirling Dervishes*. Albany, N.Y.: State University of New York Press, 1992.

Morgan, Lawrence. *Flute of Sand—Experiences with the Mysterious Ouled Naïl*. London: Odhams Press Limited, 1956.

Rees-Denis, Paulette. *Tribal Vision: A Celebration of Life through Tribal Belly Dance*. Portland, Ore.: Cultivator Press, 2008

Sachs, Curt. *World History of the Dance*. London: Allen & Unwin, 1938.

Said, Edward. *Orientalism*. London: Routledge & Kegan Paul, 1978.

FURTHER RESOURCES

Videography

Authentic Dance

Adam Basma Middle Eastern Dance Co.: Live In Concert
   Great example of dabkeh performance

Fifi Abdo Concert in al Esmailia
   Performance by a very famous Egyptian belly dancer

Hahbi 'Ru Live!
   Folkloric-style belly dancing and line dances

Iraqi Variety Folk Dances
   A large folkloric troupe performing Iraqi dances

Mezdeke Show and Super Oriental
   Turkish belly dance performances

Rare Glimpses by Ibrahim Farrah, prod. by Andrea Breeman, 56 minutes, 1994.
   Includes very early (1897) footage of a dancer, a real Guedra, the Lebanese dancer Nadia Gamal

Authentic Dance Performance in an American Movie

Valley of the Kings
   A 1954 movie starring Robert Taylor and Eleanor Parker, includes a brief dance performance by Samia Gamal with real Egyptian music and dancers

Instructional Videos

Amaya's Gypsy Fire!
   The connections among Gypsy, Arabic, and Flamenco dances

American Tribal Style Belly Dance, Volume 1
Instructional video taught by Kajira Djoumahn

Balancing Act
Sword and candle dancing taught by Mezdulene

Bellydance Live, Part 3—Folkloric Dance
Instructional video taught by Keti Sharif

Bellydance! Magical Motion
Instructional video taught by Atéa

Egyptian Drum Solo Choreography, Volume 1
Advanced level—Jamilla Al-Wahid

Floor Work Made Simple
Instructional video taught by Mahisha

How to Play Finger Cymbals with Mesmera
Instructional video taught by Mesmera

Morocco & the Casbah Dance Experience: Riverside Dance Festival, Morocco's #1 Video and Folk Dances of Egypt, Nubia, and the Sudan, Morocco's #6 Video The Dancer's Toolkit
Instructional video taught by Bàraka

Tribal Basics Volume 1: Dance Fundamentals (Revised)
Instructional video taught by Carolena Nericcio

Veil and Arm Dancing by Amaya
Instructional video taught by Amaya

Middle Eastern Instruments and Rhythms

Bellydance Live, Part 1—Introduction to Music & Rhythms
Instructional video taught by Keti Sharif

WEB SITES

The Art of Middle Eastern Dance by Shira
http://www.shira.net/
This Web site includes information on frequently asked questions, books and videos, reviews, an introduction to belly dancing, and links to teachers and performers throughout the world.

Authentic Dance on YouTube
http://www.youtube.com

This site includes vintage footage of many of the major dance stars mentioned in this book—as well as performances of countless other wonderful dancers.

Aziza Sa'id's Mid-Eastern Belly Dance Site

http://www.ZillTech.com

This Web site that includes information for beginners, online dance lessons, books and videos, and links.

Belly Dance Directory

http://www.bhuz.com

This is the largest online belly dance community, with forums, events, news, and blogs.

Discover Belly Dance

http://www.discoverbellydance.com

This Web site includes costumes, videos, belly dance classes, and instructor information.

The International Academy of Middle Eastern Dance

http://www.bellydance.org

IAMED is an international association of belly dancers, belly dance instructors, choreographers, and musicians dedicated to promoting belly dancing. The site includes DVDs for sale, photographs, events, and links.

Official site of dancer, choreographer, and instructor Suhaila Salimpour

http://www.suhailainternational.com/

This site features online classes, certification information, a newsletter, and workshops.

Yasmina's Joy of Bellydancing

http://www.joyofbellydancing.com

Here is a comprehensive Web site that includes information on the history of belly dancing, costumes, books, videos, links, directory, and reviews.

PICTURE CREDITS

INDEX

ABOUT THE AUTHOR AND CONSULTING EDITOR

Author **Penni AlZayer** is an arts educator who has traveled extensively in the Middle East and Europe and lived in the Arabian Gulf region for 13 years. She is married to a Saudi professor (an artist and actor) and is the mother of four. When she is not in Riyadh, she resides in McArthur, Ohio, where she hopes to continue to dance and share the gift of Middle Eastern dance for many more years.

Consulting editor **Elizabeth A. Hanley** is Associate Professor Emerita of Kinesiology at the Pennsylvania State University. She holds a BS in Physical Education from the University of Maryland and an MS in Physical Education from Penn State, where she taught such courses as modern dance, figure skating, international folk dance, square and contra dance, and ballroom dance. She is the founder and former director of the Penn State International Dance Ensemble and has served as the coordinator of the dance workshop at the International Olympic Academy, in Olympia, Greece.